V O L U M E T W O

LADIES *of*
GOLD

THE REMARKABLE MINISTRY OF THE GOLDEN CANDLESTICK

The Authorized Compilation by
J A M E S M A L O N E Y

WESTBOW
PRESS®
A DIVISION OF THOMAS NELSON
& ZONDERVAN

WestBow Press books may be ordered through booksellers or by contacting:

WestBow Press
A Division of Thomas Nelson & Zondervan
1663 Liberty Drive
Bloomington, IN 47403
www.westbowpress.com
1 (866) 928-1240

Because of the dynamic nature of the Internet, any web addresses or links contained in this book may have changed since publication and may no longer be valid. The views expressed in this work are solely those of the author and do not necessarily reflect the views of the publisher, and the publisher hereby disclaims any responsibility for them.

Any people depicted in stock imagery provided by Thinkstock are models, and such images are being used for illustrative purposes only.

Certain stock imagery © Thinkstock.

All scripture quotes are KJV, unless otherwise noted.

ISBN: 978-1-4497-4639-1 (sc)
ISBN: 978-1-4497-4640-7 (hbk)
ISBN: 978-1-4497-4638-4 (e)

Library of Congress Control Number: 2012906482

Print information available on the last page.

WestBow Press rev. date: 8/20/2015

CONTENTS

FOREWORD

(Read this...)

If you haven't read Volume One of *Ladies of Gold*, let me strongly urge you to do so, prior to reading this second compilation. It isn't so much that one would need to read the first part to understand the second part (although it certainly doesn't hurt.) But rather, when studying works of this nature, if one doesn't have a basic knowledge of the authors, it is quite easy to misinterpret those authors' intents. And if I may be so bold, I think the introductory chapter I wrote for Volume 1 will nicely familiarize the reader with just who the Golden Candlestick were.

Frances Metcalfe and the ladies (and some men) of the Golden Candlestick Fellowship were not your "average" Christians, whatever that means. We jokingly quip that Frances often spent more time in heaven than she did on earth, and while that's a slight overstatement, it's not as farfetched as you're probably thinking. Frances' writings were by and large literal revelations shared through an allegorical medium. What I mean by that convoluted statement is, when Frances says she was translated or raptured, she really means she was translated or raptured. Not that she had a dream or a vision of, say, the cosmos, but rather that she literally was transported to the cosmos. When she prophesies something to the extent of, "The Lord told me..." she most often means He was speaking to her face-to-face in full bodily form. There are not many "modern" seer prophets who have had the level of physical manifestations of our Lord that Frances had. It came at a price most of us are unwilling to pay, and honestly, she was specially called as a forerunner for these kinds of experiences.

That's kind of hard to swallow for most Christians, but you have to understand that Frances and her covenant group of harp-and-bowl worshipers spent hours and hours, five, six days a week, in high praise before the Throne. And I mean "before" the Throne as literally as I can. For the vast majority of us, we don't spend five hours a day praying in tongues. And that's not necessarily a "bad thing." (Although we could all stand to pray in tongues a little bit more!) We've all heard the phrase, "So heavenly minded, no earthly good." That's not to imply the Ladies of Gold fell into that category, but if we all did what Frances and the GC did, nothing would ever get accomplished here on earth.

Keep what I'm saying in balance here—you're about to read a book where the authors spent most of their time enraptured to heaven! But it was something to which they were specifically called, and while I believe Frances intended that many others were to follow her example, one must be discerning as to what the Lord is calling one to do.

While it is noble and right to pursue our Bridegroom in an ever-increasing manner, it is also noble and right to live one's life as God created it. Take care of your children, go to work, pay your mortgage, help your neighbors, and love the Lord with all your heart, soul, mind and strength. And if He bestows the kind of grace that made the GC so unique, then praise His name! If not, we will in no way lose our reward for being faithful in the manner He has called us.

I'm not writing this brief foreword to put a dampener on what you're about to read, but I do feel impressed to caution the reader to recognize that the Lord expects us to fulfill our earthly requirements as well. I don't want to receive a bunch of e-mails that state "we've been raptured fifteen times, but our children are always late to school and only have cold Spaghetti O's for dinner five nights a week!" That's not what Frances means when she says, we should all be pressing toward a greater revelation and manifestation of God's physical presence in our day-to-day lives.

And, as I stated in Volume 1, I don't necessarily, unequivocally agree with everything the GC taught. For the most part, they were 99.9% correct, but I believe their theology could've benefited from some strengthening in certain areas, specifically in their understanding of physical health/healing. I do not place the Apocrypha as "divinely inspired" on the same level as the written Word of God as we now have it. (Neither did Frances, but again, if you didn't know that, one might be under the misconception that the GC held the Apocrypha to the same level as the Holy Bible. I assure you they did not.)

In this modern-day Church, we are sadly seeing an alarming move toward a mixture of inclusion—it is being taught behind some pulpits that Allah and Jehovah are the same deity! It is being taught that we can "soul travel" at our own desire, apart from the Holy Spirit initiating a transcendent encounter with Him. These are heresies, these are New Age deceptions. Be wary of them, be rooted in the Word of God, be discerning. How can you do so? By remaining in the secret place with the Lord Jesus Christ—by being 100%, without fail focused on Him and what He taught in His earthly ministry, as revealed by the Bible.

I'm all for glory encounters, I'm all for transcendent, rapture experiences, subject to the written Word. I believe in this "Dove" Company Frances foresaw. I believe, for the most part, in her Latter Rain revelations. Yes, there will be a manifestation of the sons of God as we approach the final "End-Time" second advent of our Lord Jesus Christ (whenever that may happen to be.) But don't lose sight of the simplicity and perfection that is the doctrine of the Son of God in the name of "pressing into the 'new' thing."

I fervently pray we never lose sight of what Jesus Himself taught and demonstrated in His earthly ministry: saving the lost souls, cleansing the sick, healing all manner of disease, casting out the demonic forces who are desperately trying to lead us astray with these new quirky doctrines.

Neither does/did Frances and the Ladies of Gold.

Ultimately, it's not my place nor a command from the Lord that I should try and preach to everyone who reads this book, attempting to make sure they understand just what Frances and the GC is trying to say in these writings. Some readers may get off on tangents that the Golden Candlestick never intended. But I trust in the Spirit. I trust in His goodness. It is He who will lead you into what is right and true concerning Himself.

But it is my responsibility to uphold and make clear what The ACTS Group International stands for. This ministry the Lord has entrusted to us is the direct extension of the Golden Candlestick—so it's important that we share with you our heritage, where we come from, and we are certainly not the end-all, be-all of a prophetic healing ministry. We are all striving toward a very high mark, we all fall short in areas, and it is only by the grace of God *any* of us accomplish anything of any lasting, eternal worth, that includes Frances Metcalfe and the Golden Candlestick!

There's lots to learn and strive for in the following pages. The rich history that is the Golden Candlestick deserves to be given to the new generation of the Bride. Come on up, Doves! Press in, you Mary-Hearts. May the grace and peace of our Lord Jesus Christ saturate your daily life. And, as He wills, let us prepare for rapture and translation! Let us praise and worship Him as we've never praised or worshiped Him before. Let us live a life of praise, let us suffer gloriously for His name's sake. Let us return to Him what He has deigned to give to us: life. It's only what is rightfully His in the first place!

—James Maloney
February 1, 2012
Argyle, Texas

THRU RAPTURE
INTO TRANSLATION
PART TWO

Frances Metcalfe

B y *faith* Enoch was translated that he should not see death, and was not found, because God had translated him; for before his translation he had this testimony, that he pleased God." (Hebrews 11:5)

"For the Lord Himself shall descend from heaven with a shout, with the voice of the archangel, and with the trump of God: and the dead in Christ shall rise first: Then we which are alive and remain shall be caught up together with them in the clouds, to meet the Lord in the air: and so shall we ever be with the Lord." (1 Thessalonians 4:16, 17)

"Behold, I show you a mystery; we shall not all sleep, but we shall all be changed." (1 Corinthians 15:51)

The revelations set forth in this booklet were given during experiences of "rapture," beginning in January, 1942, and continuing for several months. Guided by the Holy Spirit, I have made an earnest attempt to interpret these heavenly experiences in earthly language. Needless to say, the *testimony* falls far short of the *reality*.

Since the first edition was mailed out in 1943, we have received letters from other Christians, in many parts of the world, who testify to similar experiences and rejoice in the testimony recorded on these pages. By many reliable witnesses the Holy Spirit has confirmed the word given to us that "rapture"—meaning "to be caught away or transported in the spirit"—is preparatory to the even greater experiences of *transport* (in the body), and *translation*. All three of these experiences are recorded in the Word of God and are among the promises given to the full overcomers in the Latter Days, or Time of the End. A body is being prepared "as it hath pleased Him," as revealed in 1 Corinthians, 15th chapter, whose blessed privilege is to be changed and caught up *alive*—made like unto Christ, our glorious Head. Foretastes such as this booklet records are becoming more numerous as the time of the Consummation draws near.

This was the Lord's doing, and it is still marvelous in our eyes! With all praise and glory unto our Lord Jesus Christ, who has revealed Himself unto us and has shown us things to come, kindling our love, reviving our hope, confirming our faith, I offer this testimony to you.

In Part 1, which is published as a separate book, I have related how these experiences began with a surprising "catching up" into the heavenlies. In the weeks that followed, I passed through severe illness and walked in the "valley of the shadow of death" with our Lord. I was taken by Him into "The King's House" and "Garden." And there He appeared to me as the KING of glory! In order to fully understand Part 2, you should read Part 1 first. Copies are available upon request.

Yours in the love of our glorious King and Bridegroom,

—FRANCES METCALFE

ESTHER'S FEAST

My heart was filled with sorrow when I knew for certain that I must return to my natural life and family. This may seem strange; but I could not bear the thought of leaving this heavenly rest. So sweet and full was the presence of The King, and so rich the revelation, that it seemed the consummation of rapture, the full union—when we actually do put on the wedding garment, which is immortality—must be right at hand! I little realized how much further preparation I needed! Now all was interrupted and ended, and I must go back to the everyday world. How could the Lord rapture me or reveal Himself in the midst of caring for my children and housework? It was really a test of faith, for I was still very weak and my nerves were exhausted. School vacation was at hand, and with it constant responsibility and confusion. I stifled my tears, and prayed for grace. It was such a shock to leave "the King's House"! I can well realize why those who are brought back from death are seldom satisfied. I was literally all "unstrung." Indeed, I was shown that I was like a harp now being tuned to play a higher melody. What torture as the strings are stretched!

Everything natural was so foreign to my mind as to seem strange or absurd. I was truly "lost" to the world, in a new way. I found that to cease contemplating the Lord was most painful, and that I could scarcely appear even sensible outwardly. Fortunately, I really was ill, and this covered my condition somewhat. I was in for a time of testing and perfecting. This type of experience seems to increase our capacity and sensitivity to suffering in an astounding way. Oh, the grace and divine love we need to pass from rapture to torture—for such it sometimes proves to be. But, as always, the Holy Spirit comforted me, and instructed me that St. Paul was trained to be content in *any state:* Abased or exalted, in prison or in the third heaven, he was alike at rest in the perfect will of God. The Spirit will give us a beautiful, balanced, even walk, if we will let Him have His way.

Again, I must walk by *faith!* This is hard to do after we have been flooded with Divine favor, and have found a welcome in the heavenly realm, a love beyond description. Especially hard, since, before that, we had been so grievously wounded, smitten and misunderstood here in the earth. No misunderstanding there—all harmony, order, peace, unity. What rest after turmoil!

I saw that I must stay by faith in this heavenly rest, though I was outwardly greatly tried. Sweet comfort was given in this song:

> Into His royal garden The King invited me,
> Thru the golden portals He led me tenderly,
> There, amid its beauty, my soul finds sweet repose,
> Walking 'mid the lilies, communing with each rose.
> Every lovely flower speaks of heaven above,
> Every fragrant bower breathes with His pure love.
> Gladly will I tarry, and with the song birds sing,
> In His royal garden, feasting with The King.
> In His royal garden The King oft' walks with me,
> To my heart He whispers His Kingdom mysteries.
> Down each sunny pathway He leads me on His arm,
> I walk as in a dream, enraptured by His charm.
> On my ear is falling a heavenly melody,
> And my heart responds with holy rhapsody.
> Someday, in this garden, wedding bells will ring,
> In golden tones announcing my marriage to The King!

I was indeed surprised when the Holy Spirit reminded me that The King wanted me to give Him a feast! This had been coming to me since before my illness. True, I had come to The King's Feast. But what had I to offer such a one as He? Of course, I see now that the pattern was true. Ahasuerus made a great feast, a "Kingdom" feast. "Vasti," a type of the "Church" as a whole, refused to come. She was busy with a feast of her own making. The greatly offended King ordered her set aside and a new queen prepared. Many were then chosen to be prepared. This took much time. Esther fully submitted to the Eunuch in all matters, and not only pleased him, and obtained the best, but also won the love and favor of The King. After this *she* made a feast too. She so pleased the King that she won the release of all her people, and was herself greatly advanced in power. Now, since in me this "drama" of truth was being enacted, as a pattern, it was fitting that I follows Esther's example. (Book of Esther)

THE MARY HEART

I see it all so plainly now. We cannot imagine how hungry our King is to be loved and "entertained" by His dear Bride. Oh, our terrible neglect of our God! and of His Son! Of His great salvation! Yes, terrible is His neglect by the Bride. He is so hungry for our love. How He longs for a "Bethany" in your heart and mine! I began to feel a great desire in my heart to minister to Him personally, as Mary and Martha did. I was led to prepare for Him a real feast. Yes, actually! Of course, it was a Spiritual Feast, but it was outward too! How odd it all seemed to my own mind. But, as I worked, the Holy Spirit instructed me, for I was very ignorant of royal matters. I found a new devotion kindling in my soul, a jealous desire to be lost in sacrificial love. I wanted to live for the pleasure of The King alone. I wanted to lavish on Him the love He richly deserves and so deeply desires. He said to His disciples, "With desire, have I desired to eat this feast with you." Oh God, give us understanding: we are so cold and unresponsive to the deeper emotions and affections of our Lord! Give us the understanding of Mary of Bethany, a true bride—a pattern for us. I found that I was longing now to go to extremes of devotion to show Him that His bride loved Him, as women of this world often love and sacrifice for their husbands. I wanted to *lavish* love upon Him. Blessed Holy Spirit, the Bride's true Friend and Guide!

> How precious is the memory of Mary,
> Who knew and loved Thee long ago;
> Her act of love and deep devotion,
> Thy Word has caused the world to know.
> Lord, I would worship Thee as Mary,
> With a pure and fervent heart;
> Let me sit and learn at Thy feet, now,
> Choosing too, the "better part."

Lord, give me a heart, like Mary,
Broken and contrite in Thy hands,
A heart that knows and loves Thee,
A heart that truly understands.
Let me, as she, anoint Thee
With love's rare essence, pure and sweet.
I, too, would kneel in deep devotion
Low at Thy nail-scarred feet.

What a friend the Holy Spirit is to the Bridegroom too—for daily He was revealing My King to me, and instructing me about His inner desires. My King had been so modest that He had not spoken to me of His desires, but only had lavished favor upon me, as unto His Bride, the Church.

How true is the pattern: The Bride, after recovering from the first stunning revelation of love and favor, awakens at last to devotion and love and sacrifice which fairly consume her! Tirelessly she works; shamelessly she runs after Him, as depicted in The Song of Solomon. Others misjudge her, even condemn her. They attribute her desperate desire for Him to other causes; but she, all unmindful of them, hastens after her Beloved. She is tardy in her response, but none the less eager to manifest the depth of her new devotion.

I was impressed so much at this point with the delight such thoroughly devoted souls bring to the Father. An obedient child elicits love and praise and reward. But if that child goes beyond obedience, in lavishing personal attention and love upon His Son, this greatly pleases the Father. Let the Bride so ardently love The King, as to supply the great lack of love found among His people as a whole!

If the Holy Spirit brings us to this place of devotion, be sure He will provide ample crosses, sufferings and extreme tests of love. But, after this rapture, we will glory in these things, and rejoice in them with joy unspeakable. "Many waters cannot quench love, neither can the floods drown it. Love is strong as death." This love delights in all manner of *extremity* for its Lover; even as a real mother inwardly exults in the pangs of childbirth, and counts all her labor for her baby after its birth, through its long childhood, as a privilege of love. This supernatural love far surpasses any natural love, however refined. It burned in the breasts of the martyrs, and made death most sweet to them. It shall be kindled in the Bride during rapture, and never again will it flicker and die. Thus, in pre paring for this feast, you see, I actually was preparing a *love* feast. In detail I was shown the appointments and preparations, and all were an outward showing of the written Word.

Only guests well pleasing to the King may be invited to a Royal Feast, and none comes uninvited. So here, again, I sought the mind of the Spirit. Now, during the last week or so of my stay at "The King's House," the Lord began to send others in by supernatural ways. Some of these met Him in the garden before they could get to the door. One, upon entering, saw many angels, and was so overcome by the Lord as to be unable to converse for an hour or more. One by one they had come. "These are the ones to invite," the Spirit whispered.

I wondered how I could ever explain an actual "garden feast" to these dear ones, for such a thing was unheard of in our midst. But, here again, the Lord intervened. One brother was shown in a dream that he was to attend such an affair. Another sister was given a beautiful dress which seemed too elaborate for her use; but the Lord showed her she was to wear it to a feast. Others were dealt with in similar ways. Indeed, so many things happened so rapidly and in such order that we were all amazed!

This feast proved beautiful beyond words. The Song of Solomon was the theme. And one after another was moved to bring forth revelations, or portions of the Word, as we ate of the choice fruits at the table. In the King James Version, Esther's Feast was called a "banquet." This proved to be just that, in the Spirit. At its close some were anointed with ravishing music, singing in the Spirit. And so heavenly were these manifestations that all alike felt the presence of The King. The Lord graciously revealed Himself to me. He touched and strengthened my body, and gave me to understand that now all in my "realm" in the Spirit were to be brought in to share these glories. So, as for Esther, this feast became a "Purim," in which many were released to share celestial privileges! Hallelujah!

I am sure that, as each one of us is taken into these realms, we shall find that our passing in involves drawing many others after us into the heavenlies. Our "realm" in the Spirit shall be greatly blessed and enhanced. Some who were present were already being shown new and wonderful things in regard to rapture and their calling in the Bride. The Lord was moving in many directions now, and great was our joy! I returned to my home, well content to devote myself to my King in sacrificial love, even though I might never receive another divine favor here on earth. But, swiftly He moved to bring me into a higher state!

James Maloney

THE NEW EDEN

Along the celestial highway of rapture I was swiftly drawn to another mysterious portal—a gateway once barred to the sons of men, guarded by angels with flaming swords! No need to fear them now, ah no, for He who once was dead, and now is alive for evermore, is holding my hand—He who holds the keys of death and hell! At His Word the shining angels shall step aside, and I shall pass with Him, the Second Adam, into the New Eden. There He shall teach me the mysteries of the first creation. There, too, I shall learn of the glorious New Creation. I shall be shown the perfect New Eve—Bride of the Second Adam—eternal Helpmeet of creation's Head! What joy! What anticipation as the Spirit whispered these things to my heart! May He open to you, dear one, these divine revelations. For so my Lord led me, in His matchless grace; and He gave me to understand that many of His dear ones shall be finding their way past the flaming swords into this Holy Ground! Amen!

This beautiful garden of Love is for YOU!

Once, in the earth, a fair garden grew,
Eastward in Eden Land,
A garden celestial, Paradise for two,
Planted by God's own Hand!

Alas, because of sin, this garden was barred,
Closed to the sons of men;
Angels were guarding it with flaming sword,
And none might enter in.

Then, from heaven, God sent His only Son,
Made in the form of man,
And when His work on Calvary was done,
The gates were swung wide again!

This beautiful garden of love is for you,
Grown in the sunshine and watered with dew.
Each blossom is holding a promise sweet,
Each petal, a treasure to fall at your feet.

Its enchanting fragrance is borne on the air,
Its entrancing beauty is surpassing fair;
This wonderful garden, this heavenly garden,
Is a garden of Love... for you!

INTO A HIGH MOUNTAIN... APART!

If only I could tell this story as it deserves to be told! If only I could sing it to you in the mystical tongue of a Seraph! Then, perhaps, this "sweetest story ever told" would inflame your heart with holy love, as my heart flamed in its unfolding. Alas, I must tell it to you in our prosaic language. May the Holy Spirit breathe upon it as you read, that you may share some of the wonder with me. Amen!

How rapidly the Lord moved in this experience of rapture!

The long waiting times, the "empty" seasons of dryness, were all passed away now in the thrilling unveiling of new revelations. From height to height... from glory to glory... this was the pattern! Immediately following "Esther's Feast," the Lord revealed to me that He was preparing to take me out of the city. I felt that to leave my home and family again would be an impossibility. But the Lord moved quickly to bring it to pass. He dealt with my two precious prayer partners along this same line. They were shown that it was His will for us to spend much time waiting on Him. While in prayer, the Lord gave me the Word regarding the calling of Peter, James and John, to come up into a "high mountain apart." We three were to come apart with Him. He also revealed to me that I was going into the heights to meet primarily with Him alone. I was commanded to "see no man, save Jesus only." He also showed me in a vision a rock altar upon the mountain top. He promised to meet me there in a new way.

I cannot describe the *awe* I felt in these divine dealings. They were so vivid, so solemn, so weighty, so supernatural, that godly fear accompanied each revelation. (This has increased as rapture has progressed. There has been much joy. But I can assure you that it is a solemn joy, sacred and profound.)

I believe I should mention here that the enemy moved in many ways in an attempt to hinder this retreat. Some imagine that in rapture the enemy never interferes, and that God moves so supernaturally that we do not have to exercise faith and obedience. Please do not be thus deceived! True, in some instances, the Lord may move so rapidly and unexpectedly that neither you nor the enemy can hinder. But, in most of these dealings, I found that I had to move as rapidly as the Lord moved. In other words, there had to be an instant and full obedience, if I was to attain all that the Lord willed. He will not take a way that is according to our own planning, for His ways are higher than our ways. In fact, His rapture ways are heavenly ways, and we are most ignorant pilgrims. If we try to reason, or argue, or plan, we shall probably hesitate long enough to temporarily interfere with God's perfect order. In all of these dealings there is a time element. In every case God moves ahead of the enemy. At times it has seemed to me like a breathtaking race to outrun the opposing forces. I don't believe I can stress too much the need of faith and obedience in these supernatural experiences. Your enemy will still try to hinder and deceive you, and you dare not heed any voice, save the voice of the Lord! There is no time to lose! The highway of rapture is not for those who hesitate and doubt.

However, even though this is all true, I was given renewed grace and strength to believe God and to quickly obey. Hitherto, I had often been delayed and hindered by the enemy; but now I found that in every case he was absolutely defeated and unable to prevent the outworking of God's perfect plan, even though he often made fierce and sudden assaults. Praise our God! It seems that after we enter into this way of rapture by divine love, having already passed through a "Job" experience, we get to the place where we can say with him: "I have heard of Thee with the hearing of my ear, but now, my eye seeth Thee!... I know Thou canst do all things, and that no purpose of Thine can be restrained!" (Job 42:2,5) I have found this to be true over and over again. The "impossible," the "unheard of," becomes the reality. Often we have said: "There is nothing too hard for the Lord." Now we begin to *see* it as well as *say* it!

So our enemy did all that he was permitted to do to hinder our departure but, nevertheless, on the appointed day we were on the road and were being taken swiftly, in "the King's chariot," to "The King's Mountain Garden." We had many trials along the way, delays and hindrances. But in all these things we saw a spiritual lesson, and continued to praise and sing. Before we reached our destination, I began to be very ill, and I bear witness that the last few miles of the way were the longest, steepest and hardest miles of the road. The Lord had chosen to take us to one of the most beautiful National Parks noted for its grandeur and primitive beauty. It would be hard to surpass anywhere in the world! Yet, here is a strange thing about it—not until you have reached the very *top,* can you glimpse any of its glory! In fact, the last few miles are so steep and barren that I could scarcely believe any such wonder land existed within a radius of a thousand miles! I tell you this for the encouragement of some who may be traveling the last long steep climb to the top of the mountain, where they will see the sunrise of the New Day. Take courage! Some of the watchmen upon the mountaintop have seen the first glimpses of the Sun of Righteousness, as He arises with healing in His Wings! They are calling to you: "Come up higher, come up to the Mount of Transfiguration! Your King is waiting for you upon the mountaintop!"

THE NEW PROMISED LAND

But, at length, we traversed the last mile of the way! By this time I was really very ill. The altitude was high, and my heart was fairly pounding. I felt that at any moment I would faint. We were all exhausted, and there was no natural cause for the exhilaration I shortly experienced. The moment I stepped out of the car, and my feet touched the ground, I found a strange thing happening to me. Let me try to describe it.

The air, which was very balmy and fragrant, produced an effect in me like the drinking of strong wine. As I breathed deeply, it became the very *breath of God* to me, the breath that breathed over Eden, the breath by which the first man became a living soul, the divine breath by which the Second Adam became a life-giving Spirit. He was raised from the dead by the breath of the Almighty! This air, which did seem the very breath of the Father to me, almost instantly strengthened me, and I began to feel most wonderfully *alive* and most deliciously *intoxicated.* I felt *renewed:* body, soul and spirit— revived, quickened, and exultant! My heart seemed to cry out: "Oh, I am breathing air from a new realm. I am getting 'second' wind!"

As my feet touched this new high ground, it appeared to me that I was walking on foreign soil. In some way that I cannot account for, my feet would barely touch the ground, and then spring up off it. I actually felt that I had "hind's feet." O, it was most delightful, and I seemed to be passing out of myself entirely into the Lord, who was now revealing Himself to me as Creator. Everywhere I looked I saw Him! Creation's Lord! The mammoth trees, the flowers, the birds, in fact, everything He had made on which my eye came to rest spoke to me of Him in an unuttered word. I was like a child, dazed with wonder, for I was looking at the natural creation, as though I had never seen it before!

How can I clarify this experience to you? Let me say that I have always loved the beauties of nature, and have been inspired by them to worship and love the Creator. But this was another thing entirely. I felt that I was completely lost in the Creator of the creation. Everything created was revealed to me as a living Word of God. It was as St. Paul said:

"For the invisible things of Him from the creation of the world are clearly seen, being understood by the things that are made; even His eternal power and Godhead." (Romans 1:20, King James) The Amplified New Testament says: "For ever since the creation of the world His invisible nature and attributes, that is, His eternal power and divinity have been made intelligible and clearly discernible in and through the things that have been made—His handiworks."

As I looked at the visible creation, the invisible things of God appeared to me, unveiled, and everything I beheld became a Word of God. For I saw that all things made had been created by the Word of God! I felt, too, that the creative Word of God was very near me, even in my mouth. Then I knew, beyond any doubt, that the *sons of God* will be given this *creative Word!* Not only shall the curse of the present creation be lifted; but to them also shall be given the joy of co-acting with the Father in the creation of the New Heaven and Earth! In a word, I felt "at one" with God in His creation—not as the pagan is at one with nature as God; but as the sons of God are at one with the Father, and are rulers over all the works of His hands!

It has taken several minutes to recount this experience, but it all took place within a few moments. In fact it just happened all at once! This was most surely another type of rapture. For from that moment I lost all trace of sickness, weariness, heaviness and discomfort. During the eight days spent upon this mountaintop, I averaged only about three hours sleep a day, if that much. I never really grew tired nor seemed conscious of discomforts. I was living in another realm, and the memory of the things of this present world could be recalled only with effort. I also felt that I had entirely lost my identity—so completely was I identified with my Lord. He was revealed to me now, not as the King, the greater than Solomon, but as "Elohim." "In the beginning Elohim created heaven and earth." "Oh, the matchless names He bears, and the forms of love He wears!"

Whatever the type of rapture, I have found that always, if it is complete, it takes me out of *myself*—out of my own mind and ways, and even out of my identity at times. I am not conscious of myself as an individual, but only as a part of this wonderful Body, "hidden away with Christ in God." Thus there is no sense of personal satisfaction or elation in the reception of these divine favors. Even though most wonderful and profound mysteries are revealed, even though the Lord may speak to us great things and pronounce unusual favors and blessings, we do not receive these things as unto our *self.* In fact, self does not enter at all into these celestial affairs. Oh, great is this deliverance from our worst enemy, even our own self! While here in the earth we must constantly watch and be on guard, lest SELF defraud God and assert prerogatives over our will. However, while in the state of complete rapture, self is temporarily inactive, and for a time we are lost in God. The longest sustained period of rapture I have experienced was during this eight days. Night and day I was free from duties and interruptions, and I lived in constant communion with the Lord in the Spirit.

MY BELOVED ON THE MOUNTAINS OF BETHER

My prayer-partners seemed to feel a touch of this same joy in creation. We at once began likening this fair garden of God to Eden. The animals played their part in the living drama, for in this park they are tame and friendly. How good of the Lord to harmonize the outward scenes with my inward state! He really knows how to "set the stage" for His divine drama! As we were eating our dinner that first night, a deer came to our table. We ate in the open, on our porch. As he approached us, my heart cried out, "My Beloved is like a roe or a young hart upon the mountains of Bether." Yes, my Beloved was drawing very near! I could feel it! I knew that He was going to come closer to me now than ever before. I could scarcely contain my delight and anticipation. How we feasted and worshiped before the Lord. "Can this be real, can it be REAL?" Over and over I asked this question.

When I retired it was not to go to sleep. Every atom of my being was awake and quickened unto God. I was expectant—more excited than any earthly Bride-to-be I have ever known! I felt youthful, pure and *new*. It was as though I had never known sin or toil or sorrow or weariness. I was restored. Is it not recorded that in the age to come the remembrance of former things will never come into the mind? All things new! Glory to God! Often I had sung Wesley's song, "Love Divine." And this phrase particularly was ringing in my heart. "Second Adam from above, reinstate us in Thy love."

Now I felt that I was reinstated. I felt that "Love-Divine" had "fixed in me His humble dwelling," and that He was coming into me in the fulness of love. I was being swept out, as by a strong tide, into the depths of that mighty ocean. Some have said that they felt they would die under such ecstasy, and prayed that It be lessened. I felt to pray that *my capacity be enlarged,* that I might be filled "with all the fulness of God" according to. the prayer of St. Paul. I actually felt that my heart *was* being enlarged or dilated to make room for a new influx of divine love. I remembered that David too prayed, "Enlarge my heart, O God." All the night long this "flooding" continued. Several times I seemed to be lifted off the bed, and experienced certain involuntary movements in my body, which I have since learned are the beginnings of the moving of the Spirit to *transport* our bodies from place to place, and finally to *translate* them.

The heavens were opening upon my soul in such a way that I felt at any moment I would be literally swept away—outward and upward to glory! It was truly wonderful, and beyond words to describe; and only a little before morning did it lessen enough to permit me to sleep. This joy continued, in a more moderate form, all during the next morning. I tried to explain to my friends this that was happening within me. But I was checked by the Spirit, and shown that I was not to reveal much at the time. We feasted on the Word of God more than on our prepared meals. But even the natural food seemed to take on a spiritual quality. Each meal became a real feast, and our relish for the written Word was most keen. We rejoiced over it, "as one that findeth great spoil." "Thy Word was found, and I did eat it, and Thy Word was unto me the joy and rejoicing of my heart, for I am called by Thy Name, O Lord of Hosts." At times I actually seemed to devour the Word.

May I say that genuine experiences of "rapture" always lead one to a greater love and appreciation for the written Word. The Lord reveals that this will invariably be the case, if our experience is of God. He warns me against any experience which tends to lessen our regard for the written Word. Years ago I was led to pray, as did David, "O Lord, lead me in a plain path, because of mine enemies. Order my steps in *Thy Word.*" This He has done consistently and, even in rapture, the Word becomes substance and is a *Living Word,* incarnate in us. Yes, even here, the written Word ever substantiates the experience. However, many revelations are given beyond that which is written—but these are always in perfect *accord* with the Word, providing we interpret it by the Spirit of God and not by the traditions of men.

As this precious day—the first day spent in the heights—continued, I found a gradual lessening of joy, and there was a growing pain or grief in my heart. This was hard to understand, for we were constantly praising God. Yet I felt wounded, sorely hurt in heart. "Something must be wrong," an inward voice would whisper, "I have failed and grieved the Lord in some way." O, how sensitive rapture makes us to the Beloved One! How quickly we sense His pleasure or grief! If He is grieved with us it seems almost unbearable. Even the slightest hurt to Him pierces us for days. Thank God for this sensitivity to Divinity! At length I saw that I must withdraw from my prayer-partners, and seek the Lord alone. I must find out from Him how I had offended. He quickly answered my prayer. "I told you to seek Me *alone*," He whispered in my heart, "I showed you an altar of sacrifice, where I would meet with you, and yet you have not sought to find it."

O, how negligent, how careless of me! In the excitement I had quite forgotten this solemn charge. I prayed to know where this altar might be found, and when I should meet with Him there. Then, to my surprise, He told me that I was to arise and go out to meet Him at the dawn! I can't tell you how difficult this seemed to me, to get up in the dark, to disturb my friends, and then to go out into the mountains alone. Yet nothing is too hard for *love!* Love alone can do *all things,* and *never faileth.* But the others—would they understand, would they not be grieved that I desired to withdraw from them? This question troubled me much, for they were not being dealt with in this way, and saw only that we were to pray in unity.

Yet, in all of this, the pattern was true. The Bride, quickened by the pulsations of the Bridegroom's love, arises *early,* before the dawn; she leaves those she loves behind, and flees away out of the night shadows into the dawn of the *New Day!* She is the first to meet Him on the Mountaintop! This divine drama, this living truth, was being enacted in me by the Holy Spirit. And, praise God! He made the writing true.

O, the wonder of it! The First Covenant, written on tablets of stone! The Second (new) Covenant, written on the fleshly tablets of the heart! The Lord commanded the prophet to *"Write the vision,* and make it plain upon tablets, that he may *run* that readeth it; for the vision is yet for an appointed time!" In this latter day, praise God, the *vision* is being written in *your heart,* and *mine,* and *enacted in our lives,* that it may be plain. Praise God, those who are able to read it *run,* and obtain the prize!

> Lord, give me a heart like Thine, I pray,
> A new heart, tender and pure;
> On its fleshly tablets engrave Thy holy Word,
> And make each writing deep and sure!
> Then take it and seal it for Thy courts above,
> With the seal of Thy Love divine,
> O, Sacred Heart, of my God and King
> Give me a heart like Thine!

THE NEW DAY DAWNS

When I told my prayer-partners that I must arise early and leave them to seek the Lord, they were a little surprised, and wondered if they should not accompany me. But I told them that I must go out *alone*. I could scarcely wait for the morning to come. All night long I again lay lost in God—expectant of a new and wonderful revelation of Himself. At times great surges of despair and doubt would roll over my soul; fear that I should fail and someway miss this holy meeting. I dared not fall asleep, lest I fail to awaken before the dawn. It was truly an all-night watch—and I "watched for Him, more than they who watch for the morning." When the time to arise finally came, Satan did much to hinder me. He beset me in various ways. He tried to convince me that all this was sheer delusion, madness, foolishness, or worse! I would surely get lost or get hurt or grow ill—in fact I might even die out there all alone in the mountains. Surely I owed it to myself, my family, my loved ones, to be a little sensible, a little less extreme and so on and on. Do you recognize his tactics?

But, by God's grace, I did arise and make my way out to seek for my Beloved. He did not appear at once, but tested me, and my heart was gripped with desperate desire to meet Him—an almost frantic devotion. Truly He desires a bride as eager to meet with Him as He was to meet with her, when He laid aside His glory and descended, out of ineffable light, into the darkness of this world of sin. We have a fervent, eager, divinely passionate *Lover,* in our God! Oh that we might grasp this truth, and that we in turn might respond with a like-love, as we arise to run after Him. Women of the world are no longer ashamed to "run after" the men of their choice; but how slow is the holy Bride of God to *run after her Lover Divine!* Yes, in my agony of heart, that holy morning, I saw these truths in a new way;

they were written on my heart, deeply, painfully. "Deep truths are dearly won," some saint has said. It is true!

I cried unto Him that morning with all the intensity of devotion of which God made me capable. And, suddenly, He *appeared!* When I say appeared, I mean *just that.* I saw Him! I touched Him! I talked with Him face to face, not as a King, not as a Creator, not as the Son of God, but, to my surprise, as the *Son of Man!* In condescension my Lord came thus to me, in humility, in kindness, in tender love. As a *man,* I could approach Him. I could draw very near Him, and not be overawed. Later I was shown how much He loves His office as *Son of Man!* Indeed He referred to Himself—as recorded in the Gospels—by this name, more than by any other. Also, in connection with His Second Advent, He said "And ye shall see the *Son of Man* coming." He refers also to His sign in the heavens at that time, as *"The sign of the Son of Man."* Herein lies a mystery; may God open it to your heart! Oh how He loves mankind! How He delights to identify Himself with humanity! Bless His wonderful Name forever! The dear Son of God who became the Son of Man, that the sons of men might become the *sons of God.*

Yes, I saw Him as a *man,* as perfect Man, the Second Adam. Not until I saw Him did I fully understand what God had meant man, made in His image, to be. Just a tender look from His eyes seemed to establish me in the grace of the pristine purity of Eve before the fall. I walked with Him through the dew-sprinkled morning, and He personally led me to the altar He had shown to me before I left the city. As we walked, He talked with me, and I lost all consciousness of a world of sin, warring in violence. I forgot that I was a mature, married woman, a mother of children. I felt what St. Paul meant when he said, speaking of the Bride of Christ: "I have betrothed thee, as a *chaste virgin.*" The chastity and purity of true virginity were revealed to me that morning, as I walked with the One altogether *pure.* O, the beauty of the first Eve! Praise God for the incorruptible beauty of the *second* Eve—Bride of the Second Adam! This glorious creature lived in *me* that morning! I was washed, purified, chaste, and I was betrothed! This was all I knew, all I could think of, all that mattered! Do you see that for the moment I was portraying the Bride—indeed I was lost in her, and she was lost in Him!

The altar to which He led me was very high, and afforded a view of the valley behind—the valley through which we had journeyed as we ascended. He reviewed to my mind all the way He had led me since first I had given myself entirely to Him. Someway, it all lived before me, in its fulness, and I was given understanding of all His dealings. That which before had been obscure, was all made plain. I had often sung, "Someday, He'll make it plain to me. Someday, when I His face shall see." Now, I saw, as from the other side, the heavenly side—and I was glad! I was comforted, happy, amazed—and filled with rejoicing. How clearly I realized that every trial, every *smallest thing,* is observed and treasured in His heart. He knows about every trace of suffering, and shares it with us.

Then, gently He turned me around and unveiled to me the land which was lying ahead! Range after range, the mountains spread before my vision. Much land ahead to be possessed! New land, rich verdant land—heavenly land. I think I felt a little as Moses felt when he viewed the Promised Land. The Lord has revealed to me that, in taking some of us into this way of rapture, we are spying out the land, foretasting of its glories—first partakers of its fruits but only *tasting*—not fully *possessing. The full possession* is for a *full company.* The Sons-of-God-Bride-Company must be caught up together, and enter into full possession in unity. Some of us may go ahead to spy and report, but we shall only taste in part. The fulness is for the appointed number, at the appointed time!

As I stood with Him that morning on the mountain top, I felt that I was the most highly favored soul who had ever lived. Nevertheless, I was shown that so rich is He, so great are His possessions, that

His privilege and favors shall be sufficient for the great company forming His Bride. I seemed to see that each one, upon entering into their possessions in Christ, would feel as I felt that day. Each will feel that the Kingdom and blessings they receive surpass all others. How rich is our God! I believe I felt much as Eve felt, when she realized that Adam's love was all directed toward her, and that the world was her kingdom. My Beloved was mine and I was His. The universe was our Kingdom. The earth seemed the merest matter, nothing but a footstool for Him. As He unveiled to me the unknown worlds of the universe, I was dazed with the magnitude of the creation. I turned from this revelation to the contemplation of His personal beauty of heart and face and, after a time, with much reluctance, I left Him to return to our cabin, rejoicing that He had promised to meet me again at sunrise.

As I departed and started on my way, lost in this new found love, I was greatly startled when suddenly another appeared to me—none else than Satan! Just as clearly and as plainly as I had seen my Lord, I saw this other one, appearing also in *the form of a man!* The sight of him turned my joy to horror. How could it be that he too was present in this Eden, lurking so very near the path I must take to return. Ah, but it was true, was it not, that Satan walked in that first Eden, and beguiled Eve? Was I to encounter him also, and must I, in the second Eve, overcome his subtlety? "Beware," said St. Paul, "that the serpent does not beguile you through his subtlety." I greatly feared; but at this time Satan was not permitted to approach me or speak to me. Had he done so, in the form of a man, I believe I should have been terrified. I was conscious that the Father was protecting me, and I seemed to have a "veil" or covering over me, which hid me from his eyes.

You may wonder just what I mean when I say that both our Lord Jesus Christ and Satan appeared to me in the form of a man. I really don't know how to enlarge upon this explanation. I saw them apparently just as I would see you, if you came into my presence. Yet I am sure I did not see them with my "natural" eyes, nor did I see an apparition. They had a body, and were substance, and not spirit alone. The only explanation I have to offer is that I was in a state of rapture, where my natural senses were almost suspended, and my spiritual senses were quickened and active in a greater degree than I had ever experienced. I was in the body, yet not in the body senses. This is as clearly as I can explain this experience, which continued off and on for many days, and has occurred at other times also.

THE PLEASURES OF PARADISE

I fairly "flew" back to our cabin, which was quite a distance from this altar. All along the way, the flowers and birds and trees shouted before me of my Beloved; indeed it seemed that all the trees of the woods were clapping their hands with joy. Not until I saw my friends did I realize how late the morning had grown, and how very long I had been away from them. Indeed, while in a state of rapture, I have no sense of *time* whatever. Though they were most gracious, I could see that they did not quite understand, and I was somewhat abashed. I found that my lips were sealed, and I had no words to tell them of His appearing. A sacred silence settled down upon me. It is still difficult to reveal these intimate, holy dealings of the Lord, and only because of divine compulsion am I able to make such an attempt. Any touch of the carnal mind upon these things seems like profanation.

Yes, my heart, soul, mind and mouth were alike hushed in awe and wonder. We ate our delayed breakfast in the glory of the sunlight of the *New Day* and, to my amazement, our brother was anointed to read the Word, and by it a confirmation was given of the experience of the morning. He read for about two hours, and by turns his wife and I laughed, cried and praised the Lord. Oh it was a feast and I marveled at the perfect witness given in the written Word. It is good to linger long at meat and wine, when one sits at the table with the King!

Then we were led to go out and gaze upon the beauties of this wonderland. Here again we laughed and shouted and cried, for everything spoke to us of our Lord and His Word. We were like excited children running from one to another, discovering a new wonder at every turn. I think that we were feeling a little touch of the delight our first parents felt, as together they explored that first garden of God. At length we came to a beautiful outdoor chapel, set in an ideal location. It was equipped with an altar and a piano, which was set in a hollow tree. (In this park the largest trees in the world are found.) I could scarcely wait to get to the keys of that piano. And when I did, I was anointed to play and sing with a power and beauty I have seldom experienced. We all sang together in deep devotion, and I felt that gradually every part of my being was being tuned, and was vibrating like a harp. I was restrung, and in tune, and the hand of the Master Musician was plucking from my strings a melody divine!

> It is My hands, love, that tune thy strings,
> And thy whole being awakes and sings,
> And as I pluck out each lovely melody,
> My heart responds, too, with heaven's harmony.
> It is My fingers, that strike the chords,
> And oh what rapture the song affords!
> Throughout the ages of My Eternity,
> I'll play on thee
> A melody divine!

Ah, this is rapture indeed! I can imagine no greater bliss in heaven than to blend with the angels and the redeemed in celestial canticles. I heard the angels singing with me, and our song came up even to the Throne, and drifted out to the utmost realms of the heavenlies. Then I was rather startled, when I suddenly became aware that others were gathering about us, listening and watching us. One young girl was regarding me with surprise. I remember looking at her as though I were in a dream and thinking, "She must be an earthly being, she looks so different from these other beings." Then I came out—enough to realize that I was still on earth myself, and was regarding a fellow-being. This girl began to laugh. "I was asleep up there on a rock," she said, "and I woke up and heard the singing coming up out of the top of the tree. It sounded so unreal,

I thought that I had died and was in heaven hearing the angels singing." We gave her, and a few others, a short testimony, and withdrew; it seemed almost unbearable to mix with people in a natural way, during this rapture time.

Upon retiring that night, I was again swept out in the Spirit, and the heavens opened upon me and seemed to be "raining" down into my soul. I saw the New Jerusalem at a distance, and the gates were open wide. Out of them streamed the golden supernal light of the Heavenly City. I saw a great company of pilgrims passing up a highway into Zion. One by one they entered the City. I found that the 84th Psalm was welling up in my heart. Then I saw myself nearing the gate and I was filled with great rejoicing. I was not actually taken into the City, however, at that time.

I also saw many other heavenly scenes, heard angelic music, and looked upon celestial beings. Their purity, devotion and beauty thrilled me, and I found a strong love for them rising in my heart. What friends to us are these ministering spirits! How they do love us, the heirs of salvation! But I found them to be very jealous about our Lord. So jealous, in fact, that unless in all things, and at all times, we glorify Him and give Him all the honor, they are apt to be somewhat aloof. However, when we begin to praise and glorify Him and tell of our love for Him, extolling His grace, then they break forth in a chorus of praise, their faces wreathed with smiles. I gradually learned how to address them, and how to recognize their ranks and stations. What strange society for a mortal to enter! How ignorant and crude I felt in the midst of their perfect order!

I could scarcely wait for the approach of dawn, so eager was I to arise and go to my Beloved. But again my heart was smitten with fear lest I never see Him again or fail, and miss His best for me. Again the enemy beset me with grievous attacks which caused my body to tremble, and my heart to faint.

The way to the mountain top to keep the sunrise tryst with God is not made easy for the Bride. The Father permits her love to be tested at every point, and not until she becomes desperate, relentless in her pursuit of her Bridegroom, does He permit her to enter the New Day! But, again, the Lord was victor. And I arose, very weak, and went out into the dawn.

This morning I was led to the little altar in the chapel. Here, in a "church" made by God's own hands—a type of that building not made with hands, eternal in the heavens—I was called to appear before the Father, and there to enter into a new relationship with Him and with His Son. So vivid and real was this dealing, so solemn this compact, that it became the most significant day of this whole mountain top experience. Angels witnessed, and rejoiced with me, and bore me away into such heavenly rapture that it seemed that my body would of necessity follow my soul and spirit in their flight. I felt that at any moment I would be *translated!* But the consummation day was not at hand, though to me it seemed it must surely be near. O hasten the day! And at this point I must draw the curtain, for much that transpired during this day would not be expedient, or even possible to utter. Truly, "eye hath not seen, ear hath not heard, neither hath it entered into the heart of man; the things which God hath prepared for them that love Him; but God hath revealed them unto us by His Spirit."

> At the breaking of the day I meet Him,
> In the glory of the rising sun,
> With great joy my heart awakes to greet Him,
> 'Ere the new day has its race begun!
> In the radiant golden dawn we walk together,
> And all life's shadows flee away,
> What a privilege is mine,
> What a rapture divine
> To meet Him at the breaking of day!

THE MOUNT OF TRANSFIGURATION

"That which we have seen and heard declare we unto you, that ye also may have fellowship with us; and truly our fellowship is with the Father, and with His Son Jesus Christ, and these things write we unto you, that your joy may be full."

How shall I tell you of the experiences which followed, as this mountain became to me a very "Mount of Transfiguration"? Truly before my eyes, my Lord was transfigured. And I, too, tasted of transfiguration.

In the preceding chapter, I described a wonderful "crowning" day which was spent in rapture and revelation. Several times during that day my own body appeared to me to be changed. It seemed to be a partially glorified body. I felt *alive* and *glowing* with strength and power hitherto untasted. (Remember that just a few short weeks back I lay at the point of death.) Now *it* seemed that I had drunk deeply of the elixir of eternal life. And it seemed that even my body had put on immortality. At the time I had no idea that I was only "tasting" of the things to come, that I was seeing a little preview of the glorious things prepared by our God for the Sons of God, the Daughters of Zion. Now I can well understand the longing Peter felt to build tabernacles and stay up on the Mount. Once, at least, during this time, the eyes of another were opened to see me in a glorified body for a few moments. I was astounded that *all* did not see it. My whole body seemed filled with light during this time.

The night which followed this glorious third day was blest with heavenly visions. These appeared to me as pictures suspended before my open eyes—colored pictures in the third dimension. I saw scenes of grandeur indescribable. If such scenes exist on the earth, I have never beheld them nor pictures of them. I believe I was seeing the world as God made it in its Edenic state before the fall. Not only was the garden of Eden garnished by God, but the whole world was a paradise of pristine beauty. I was swept out of myself completely as the Lord took me on this "world tour," a world unspoiled by the curse.

But, again, the hour before the dawn was most dark. Gradually the visions of the Spirit faded away and then, very suddenly, Satan attacked! It seemed that the hosts of darkness gathered around me, encircling me as a prey. So terrific was this attack that it awoke my friends and set them praying. At length the Spirit resisted the devil, and so great was the shaking that not only did my bed shake, but the entire cabin shook under the clash of the two realms. We were shown that the powers of the heavens were being shaken, and that the seats of the evil realms were being overturned. As Isaiah said, "I saw them fall as ripe figs." At length this battle subsided; but it left me very weak. The hour of dawn was at hand, and under great pressure and opposition I arose, by His grace, to make my way to the altar.

PARADISE LOST

What a strange world greeted me in the first rays of the morning! It no longer appeared beautiful and radiant and harmonious. It was weird, ghastly and unreal to my eyes. I found myself actually running along the road, as though fleeing from some pursuer. My heart was in the grip of a nameless fear and dread. Nature, no longer friendly to me, actually seemed an enemy. The bird's song was no longer a melody of love, but a taunting accusation! So real was my anguish, that I am unable to describe the horror of this experience. "What terrible thing has happened?" I cried, "Where is my Lord?"

Then I saw that I was like "Eve" cast out of Eden, fleeing the wrath of God and the angel's flaming sword! How could such a thing be? What had I done to be cast out, to be taken from the heights of blessing into a chasm of despair? I tried to pray, but could not cease running—indeed this running was so rapid, and over such a steep road, that in my natural strength it would have been a sheer impossibility. It was one instance of being "transported" by the Spirit. The other instances were pleasant—this most terrifying! So I ran, and cried as I ran, but the Lord did not answer my cries. "Surely He will appear at any moment," I kept telling myself, "He will end this nightmare." But no answering voice spoke to my aching heart. I felt alone in a way I have never experienced. Indeed I know now that I tasted the grief of Eve when, cast out of Paradise, she grieved more than the loss of the garden, the loss of her communion with her Creator. Without Jesus the most beautiful Eden would be a barren wilderness to His Bride! With Jesus the wilderness blossoms and sings, and the streams of life flow through the desert. Amen!

However at the time, I did not understand the strange dealing of my Lord. Why was He thus seemingly torturing my heart? "Love asks no questions," someone has aptly said. The Bride, as she advances in rapture, learns never to question God, even for a moment. She dare not reason, she dare not doubt. Hers must be a love that never fails. This love that beareth... hopeth... believeth... endureth *all* things, keeps her safely on "the more excellent way," the highway to the Throne! The redeemed pass over this King's Highway and come with singing into Zion.

I found no answer to my heart-cry from God; but Satan was quick to respond. How his voice clamored in my ears as I ran! Accusing, mocking, deriding... not *me*, but my God! But I dared not stop to answer him. I must hasten on to the altar and cast myself at the Feet of the Father. I must find out from Him, directly, what I had done to cause Him to cut me off from the heavenlies, and to banish me from His presence. I felt—as indeed my mother, Eve, must have felt—utterly graceless and without hope. But I knew, as she could not have known, the One "full of *grace* and *truth*," whose grace is eternally sufficient for me. All hell cannot shake the soul who knows in Whom he has believed, and is fully persuaded that Jesus Christ is able to keep that which has been committed unto Him. The fully committed, fully believing soul is kept by the power of God through *faith*.

This experience of rapture has brought me into a fear of God I have never known before: not a fear regarding my soul's salvation, but a fear of failing, or grieving, or displeasing the Father. I can't describe the awe I felt. For years I had seen that until the saints really fear God—in the Biblical sense of the word—sinners cannot be brought into any real fear of the Lord. I had tried to have this awe, but fell far short of it in my attitude toward God. Now, having seen the power, majesty, holiness and authority of the Trinity, I had a Godly fear of each Adorable One, which caused me to desire to perfectly obey and please them in all things. O how grievous do many of our "small" imperfections appear, the other side of the veil! God will have a perfect, faultless Bride for His Son. He is relentless in His purpose, and without partiality. She will be without spot or blemish. She will be tested to the extremity of her endurance for this high calling.

So, when I tell you that I exceedingly feared before Him, know that never for a moment did I doubt my salvation. But, if so great a one as St. John fell at His feet as dead, when Jesus appeared unto him, what effect would His appearing have upon such a weak and imperfect vessel as I? If Daniel was "sick many days" at His appearing, it is no wonder that I have been sick many times from the weight of heavenly visions. O, how unclean, how imperfect, how unworthy we feel in the midst of these divine favors. A true rapture experience *never exalts the individual...* the inevitable effect of such a revelation is to greatly humble and chasten that one. We are more apt to say with Isaiah, "Woe is me," than to say with the Pharisee, "I thank Thee that I am not as other men." I am warned of the Lord to beware of any supernatural experience which tends to exalt me or any other person, as an individual. Without exception, these true raptures exalt and glorify the Father, Son and Holy Spirit.

In this personal experience of "paradise lost," the hardest test of all this dark morning came when, try as I would, I could not find my altar in the rocks. I found the path leading up to it again and again. Satan was still besetting me. Then, someway, along the path, I would lose my way. Twice I slipped and fell several feet, sliding through thorny bushes and over rocks. Once I suffered a really hard and dangerous fall. (My clothes were torn, but no trace of injury was found on my body when I later returned to our cabin.) Finally, I gave up in sheer exhaustion. I was lost... indeed I did not even know the way back to the cabin. I could not find my altar, or my Lord! I attempted to sing and praise, but my voice choked in my throat. The previous day I had felt the most blest and favored of all creatures; this day, quite the opposite was true—I felt the most miserable and forsaken!

But divine love never fails, it is always the same. So, by His grace, I kept gasping, "Jesus, I love You, I love You. Always, in all things, in all places, I love You and trust You." Over and over I said it. I lay back, my eyes closed and, though I was all tangled up in brush and dirt, I felt sweet peace slowly flowing into my soul. I felt the presence of angels, and sang to them, telling them how favored they were that they might behold Him all the time, that they were never deprived of His presence. To my surprise they sang back to me, that I was more favored than they, since I knew Him in redemption, by grace, and was made partaker with Him of the divine nature of God. I sang and rejoiced with them. And then, suddenly, I opened my eyes and turned my head. Just above me Jesus stood, His eyes eloquent with compassion. One look into His eyes healed my heart, banished my fears, and restored my joy. I saw Him openly, plainly, as before, and again He was like unto the Son of Man.

Before He spoke, I someway knew that He had watched me every moment of this testing time, and that He had been moved with great concern and compassion. Truly our Lord is touched with the feeling of our infirmities. He is the understanding, sympathizing, Jesus! "In all their affliction He was afflicted... in His love and in His pity He redeemed them." If this was true of our God in His dealing with Israel, how much greater is His concern and pity for His chosen Bride. She is "flesh of His flesh, bone of His bone!" Nevertheless, He knows the meaning of being made perfect through suffering. If He, Son though He was, learned obedience to the Father by all He suffered, His Bride must follow Him closely in His sufferings. I felt His consuming love toward me, as a Brother-Divine. He took me gently by the hand, lifted me up, and led me to the appointed altar—which was only a few yards up the trail from the place I had fallen. Yes, He actually appeared and actually led me by the hand to the altar. I saw Him and heard Him as clearly as I would have seen you and heard you speak, had you stood there in the flesh.

PARADISE RESTORED

"You will never be able to find your way to this altar," He said, "unless I bring you here." The Bride may make a long climb, seemingly alone, assisted only by the Holy Spirit. But near the top of the mountain, the Bridegroom will *appear* and take her up the last hard climb. Once at the altar, lost in praise and worship, I clearly saw my Father's great love and wisdom in permitting this strange trial. Has not Peter warned us not to think these fiery trials strange? How quickly we forget! The Father had permitted me to taste of the bitterness and sorrow which befell Eve when, through disobedience, she lost her Eden. I could have read this story again and again. I might have heard many sermons preached about it. But not until it actually happened to me, could I have known and understood its real significance. Was it possible that I, as a bride of Christ, the Second Eve, might lose my Eden too? Had not St. Paul, in his epistle to the Corinthians, warned the chaste virgin betrothed to Christ of the subtlety of Satan? My Father wanted to teach me. So He wrote this lesson deeply in my heart and mind by letting me *experience* it.

This is the value of being brought into the *experiential state of End-Time revelation*. We may perceive many truths; but when we actually *live* these things out in experience, they are incarnated in us, never to be forgotten. So, vividly, deeply etched upon my heart, is the realization of the dangers confronting the New Eve. The loss of rank or place in the Kingdom is irretrievable. Oh how careless we are with the "true riches," toying with them often, as a child might toy with a priceless jewel. Many called, but few chosen! And only the called and chosen and *faithful* are among the full overcomers. How deadly to taste and trifle! Yes, even in a raptured state, there is danger of loss. And to whom much is given, of him much shall be required. Eve disobeyed, desiring a greater place than God had given her. (If you eat this tree you shall be as gods, knowing good and evil.) Ambition and pride cast Satan from heaven and Eve from Paradise. Be watchful, bride of Christ, and walk in humility and obedience—this was my Father's lesson and warning. Not only had He been *teaching* me a lesson, but He had been *testing* my love for the Son. The Bride's love must be a steady glow, not extinguished by the winds of adversity, "Many waters cannot quench love, neither can the floods drown it."

TWO HEARTS BEAT AS ONE

"I love You, I love You, I love You,"
This is the song of my heart.
"I love You, I love You, I love You,
I know, Lord, we never shall part.
I live by the breath of Your Spirit,
Your heart-beat is throbbing in mine.
And I love You, I love You, I love You,
My heavenly Lover-Divine."

Following this test, the love of the Bridegroom was revealed to my heart in a yet deeper manner. I felt my heart again dilating, enlarging, toward Him. He was infusing His love into my heart, and my heart was being fused with His holy heart. He showed me the difference between that which is *welded* together—and may be broken and torn apart again—and that which is fused. Each particle is so united in fusion that it cannot again be divided. Indeed, to fuse means to liquify and melt together, to blend and to unite. The Bridegroom is appearing unto His Bride now, to become fused with her, first in heart and mind and, later, in "body," when her body is glorified and made like unto His glorious Body.

O sacred union with the Sacred Heart,
What joy, what bliss, what wonderment is mine;
That He should take me into His bosom,
And hold me in the thrall of Love-divine.
O sacred union with the Sacred Heart,
To beat, to feel, to know, to love as *one*.
Ah could this be my stony heart, once broken,
Bound up... made new and whole by God's dear Son?

Oh the melting and liquidation I felt within my heart, as in the fervent heat of His consuming love, my heart was brought into full union with His heart. How much He revealed concerning His Bride, and His glorious plans for her in the days which lie ahead! These things were all far beyond my understanding. So, even as Mary, I hid them in my heart, and ponder them there.

This experience of His revelation to me as the Son of Man was all summed up by the Spirit in a poem which he moved me to write for my Beloved. He bids me share it with you. I am reluctant to speak of these intimate dealings, but He shows me that through this testimony other hearts will be moved to rise up and run after the Beloved. Some will be incited to a fervent, consuming devotion for Him. I give it to you with the prayer that you will see in it not an individual, but a "body," the precious Bride, meeting the Beloved One upon the mountaintop.

I met Him on the mountain at the breaking of the day.
The path was steep and rugged, but He led me all the way—
Led me out into the dawning, called me from my wakeful
sleep—
Far out upon a mountaintop a vigil I must keep!
(How can I sleep, when His heart is calling,
Waking my heart to a love-enthralling?)

"Rise up, my love, my dear one, rise up and come away!
Flee out of the night-shadows into the bright *new day!*
Brush sleep from thy dove's eyes, love, there's no time to

tarry,

Hasten to don thy garments; no weights with thee carry.
Swiftly upon the mountains thy hind's feet must tread,
As up to heights thou art safely led."

O, the sweetness and fragrance of the dew-sprinkled morn,
As, from the womb of eternity, a new day is born!
In the verdant trees, the bird-choir sings a paeon of praise,
As the golden clouds reflect the sun's first flaming rays;
Glorious rays, how they light up the sky,
Like fire-tipped arrows He bids them fly!

O hasten, my feet, you must *run* now to meet Him;
Keep pace with my heart, it is panting to greet Him!
He shall be as the sun when He rises in might,
On a morn without clouds, in radiant light.
As a Bridegroom He comes out of His place,
As a Strong-man, He rejoices to run a swift race.

"Step carefully now, love, there's a sharp turn to essay,
You must go by the high road, the steep, narrow way.
I'll break the trail for you, move the sharp stones aside,
For nothing shall stumble the feet of My Bride.
Ah yes, it's a hidden way, dear, and rough,
But you'll need no staff, My arm is enough!"

Be strong now, my heart, be swift and steady my feet!
I climb to meet my King, at a hidden retreat.
He's calling me up to a mountain apart,

To show me His face and to open His heart.
So long I have waited with hungering soul,
So long I have striven to reach this high goal!

O, I must not faint now, Father, help me, I pray,
Thy Word still holds promise for strength as my day.
Through years of preparation I've proved Thy sure care,
No trial was too difficult, no cross too hard to bear.
By Thy grace alone I shall reach this high goal,
And reach it I must and I *shall*, O my soul!

Now the last long ascent—the very hardest steps to take—
But He guides to the end, He never forsakes.
So up! And now, O joy surpassing, O ecstasy sublime,
I stand upon the summit, I've finished the long climb!
At last I have found a safe place to stop,
For the King has pledged to meet me here at the top.

My heart blends with my voice in a canticle of praise,
For the rising sun greets me in glory ablaze;
Such warmth, such love! Let me bask in His light,
Every shadow is behind me, banished, every trace of night!
A new world lies before me, I must conquer it too,
Higher summits are calling, a new promised land I view!

The vision blurs and fades, as tears mingle with light,
My full heart overflows—throbbing with delight.
I turn, and *there He stands,* His arms outstretched to me—
More radiant than the morning, more glorious is He.
The Sun of Righteousness, what transcendent love He
                                         brings,
Rising upon *me* with healing in His wings!

So... I met Him on the mountain, at the breaking of the day,
The path was steep and rugged, but He led me all the way;
Broke the path before me, safely kept my feet,
Scattered flowers before my steps, fragrant and sweet.
And there upon the peak, at the rising of the sun
He held me to His bosom, as the Father made us *one!*

So shall Love's old, sweet story be incarnated in the New Eve, the Bride of Christ. And through her it shall be given to a world gripped by violence and hatred. Do I appear to romanticize divine truth? This love drama of the ages has been reenacted in the *elect* of every generation. It began with a love story in the Garden of Eden: a Bridegroom, a Bride, a Paradise! It ends in another garden, the heavenly paradise of our God. In this garden there will be another Bridegroom with His holy Bride! The Song of Solomon, depicting this mysterious union, interprets it in the terms of nuptial love. This choice book has been illumined to the most devout souls throughout the centuries. Today it lives again, reenacted in us who "Kiss the Son" and running after Him cry, "Let Him kiss me with the kisses of His mouth, for Thy love is better than wine." This chaste, holy love of Christ, is the portion of the chaste, holy Bride—the "lily among thorns," the "Mary" saints, who sit long at His feet, choosing the "better part which shall not be taken away."

For her—the Bride—

Love's supernal day dawns in full glory,
And she too shall know the old, sweetest story:
At the dawn of the race, revealed to the first two;
Revealed in each age to the chosen "elect" few;
God's own secret love way, unveiling His grace,
Unveiling His nature, His heart and His face.
"God is love," hear this word ring the centuries through,
"God is love," the Bride answers, and knows it anew!

THE RIVER FROM THE THRONE

During our remaining days upon the mountaintop, many other truths were unveiled. One of the most glorious days was spent following the King's River up to its source. O, the river of the Water of Life! "The streams whereof make glad the City of God!" The river that flows from the Throne, bringing life and love and joy in its wake! How much we had thought about this river! And now an actual river was used to demonstrate this truth.

When we had first started up the long winding way to the mountaintop, we had encountered a river, and along its banks we found the only loveliness and life on that hot, barren road. The river was actually named, "King's River." Having followed it thus far, we felt moved to attempt to follow it on up to its *source*. This took us nearly a hundred miles, over a *mountaintop road*. The glories and beauties that greeted our eyes on every side were breathtaking. The primitive splendor of the scenery aroused us to a high pitch of worship and wonder. The flowers, of rare and varying types, seemed to fairly crowd along the roadside. I kept thinking of the flower-strewn path of the overcomers, as we pass over the last great highway to the Throne on the *crowning* day.

The river was at flood season, and dashed and sprayed over the rocks, much as we sing of it in the old song, "Shall We Gather at the River?" The dear sister and I stood on the bank, with the spray on our faces, and sang this song—filled with praise. In the Spirit we could see the great company of the redeemed coming up to drink at the River of Grace and to follow it to its source at the Throne. Great was our disappointment when we found that the auto road stopped short of the "head" of the river. But, since that time, in the Spirit, the Lord did take me to the Fountainhead of the River of Life—the Father, the Source. That River, the very life of the Father, will be flowing into the earth through the wide, deep, clean channels He is now preparing.

"Thou visitest the earth, and waterest it; Thou greatly enrichest it with the river of God, which is full of water. They also that dwell in the uttermost parts of the earth are afraid at Thy tokens (signs.) Thou makest the outgoings of the morning and evening to rejoice." (Ps.65)

As the time drew near for our departure from this mountain, my Mount of Transfiguration, a great solemnity overwhelmed my spirit. The weight of these revelations, and the responsibility of being entrusted with these mysteries of God, seemed more than I could bear. With this burden, my Lord added another precious one—the deep concern of His heart, HIS desire to appear, to reveal Himself, to His entire Bride company. "He appeared first unto Mary, and afterward to the eleven as they sat at meat." How great is His desire to rapture His "Mary," to reveal His love, and to perfect her for her heavenly calling. With this concern another burden gripped my soul. O, to see the manifestation of the sons of God! Of course, for years, this prayer has been in my heart; but now it flamed to a new height of intensity and fervor. O, to see His sons, formed in *His perfect image!* How clearly I saw that a *company* must be brought into these privileges. As I walked with Him, I prayed for others whom I knew were in this race, that they too might share these celestial experiences.

His last words to me, before I left the mount, were in regard to this company. He spoke to me in these words: "I have appeared unto thee for this purpose: to make thee a witness of these things which thou hast seen, and of those things in the which I will appear unto thee." (Acts 26:16) This commission brought me to a new and very heavy cross. I was staggered at the import of it, even though I rejoiced at the privilege of bearing it. The cross is the *stamp of authenticity* upon every divine experience. So my altar of revelation became for me another altar of sacrifice. Yes, deep truths are dearly won, and must be guarded at the cost of the laying down of our lives, in one way or another.

However for the time being the revelation was sealed. I was instructed to "tell no man these things," until commanded to speak by the Father. Those nearest to me knew only that which the Spirit revealed to them. I must seal my lips, even from them. A year later these experiences began to be unsealed to a few. Yet, at this time, much must still be left untold; it must remain hidden in my heart. I left the mountain top with instructions to walk in deep humility and quietness of heart. "I will confirm and establish all things in the mouths of many witnesses," spoke the Lord to me, and this He has faithfully done. I was told that I must *descend* with as much devotion and grace as had been employed in *ascending.* The Bride must be equally sure-footed and graceful in the valley as in the heights. Many, who climb rapidly and steadily on the way up, lose their balance and footing on the way down. In the experiences of rapture, we must not risk any misstep.

So I descended out of Eden, into an alien world. Yet, this did not prove to be the end, but only a new beginning. Rapture, praise God! never ends until it is consummated in Translation!

There's a new light on my pathway,
There's a new joy in my soul,
There's a new and holy rapture,
Holding me in full control.
There's a new hope to sustain me,
There's a new faith, firm and true.
For Jesus has met me
And shown me His glory,
And behold! All things are NEW!

TYPES OF RAPTURE

The Lord has impressed me to witness to you about the types of rapture I have experienced from time to time. In Part 1, I mentioned that, before leaving "The King's House," I had experienced several "rapture" dealings. I spoke of being caught up and of seeing visions in accord with The Revelation 4 and Ezekiel 1. You may wonder just what form these raptures took—whether I was in or out of the body, or in a state of trance or sleep, and whether I actually outwardly *saw* all of these things or merely *perceived* them. Just what outward effects were produced and what lasting benefits were received? So, with some reluctance, I shall endeavor to put into words many things which "are hard to be understood." May the Holy Spirit indeed now enable me to express in our poor language these divine mysteries. Bear in mind that I am testifying, and not dealing with doctrinal truth or teaching. This experience is crystal clear to me, there is no doubt at any point. But to explain it is quite another thing.

To begin with, let me say that I have found it very hard indeed to so completely abandon myself to God as to let go of every "rein." Others may not experience this difficulty. Yet I cannot believe that it shall be *easy* for anyone to pass out of the body again and again. There are many reasons for this. In the first place, our being—body, soul and spirit—three-fold yet one, is loath to be divided. The *body* offers a great resistance to everything of a supernatural nature. I have mentioned that in the Baptism of the Holy Spirit most of us encounter much resistance from our physical nature. Even after receiving this effulgence, we find that at times our body is heavy and contrary to God and, when under the influence of the carnal mind, is even at actual enmity with God. We gradually learn to submit our mind and members to the Spirit and, if we live constantly under His control, it becomes our second nature, as indeed it is, to be "in the

Spirit." However, if we disobey or walk in the fleshly mind, we find it again difficult to be under any anointing or moving of the Spirit until we are fully restored through confession.

Gradually we become accustomed to heavier and more prolonged anointings. At first a heavy anointing of intercession or prophecy or other manifestation will leave us weak and physically affected in some ways. But our bodies become more and more submitted and adjusted, until we reach the place where we may spend hours and sometimes days under a strong anointing without undue physical reaction. This is because we have become tempered and attuned to the Spirit in the physical members of our body.

Much the same is true in rapture. At first the body and the mind offer resistance and hindrance, but gradually we become yielded and can be taken in and out of the body more easily. In each case the Lord dealt with me by degrees, step by step, carefully preparing me. For He is ever loath to violate our body or mind. His operations are delicate and in harmony with our own will—never taking us beyond our will. The Holy Spirit, even in intervention, never *forces* us, but always secures the full consent of our will before acting. Evil spirits observe no such respect, and will violate our minds and bodies beyond the control of our will. Be not deceived at this point!

So interwoven is our nature that it dreads separation. The soul seems more reluctant even than the body in this matter. It fears being unclothed. As much as the body weights it, it still clings to the body, its house. When, in rapture, it is withdrawn for a short time out of the body, it feels naked, in a sense, and unprotected. O how much does this experience cause us to appreciate the house God has given us, and to say with St. Paul, "Not that I want to be unclothed, but that I long to be clothed with my house from heaven." I do not believe we shall ever completely lose this dread of nakedness until we are fully clothed upon with immortality! The spirit is the part of our being which is willing and eager to take flight unto

God from whence it came. In regeneration each of us was begotten in the Father's bosom. He is the source from whence we sprang, as the offspring of God. The spirit part of our being is ever ready to return unto its source. But so is it united with the soul that it cannot divide from it, for by it, the spirit, the soul is eternally saved through Christ. I wish I might make this as clear to you as it has been made to me.

I believe I mentioned that at one time I was "divided"—like a burnt offering—by the Holy Spirit and the "sword of the Spirit." "The Word of God is quick and powerful and sharper than any two-edged sword, piercing even to dividing asunder the joints and marrow, and the *soul* and *spirit*." Dear ones, this was a real piercing. I can't tell you how terrible it was when, for a brief moment, my spirit was cut asunder from my soul. But, in that moment, I discerned what was spirit and what was soul. Up until that time this was all obscure. It was done as a "demonstration," but was so real that for days I felt I was truly lying on that altar, cut asunder. The unredeemed will experience a permanent division when the lost soul is severed forever from the spirit, the only connection we have with God. Now, I understand the horror of "the second death"—so much greater than the loss of the body!

Let me continue further. I mentioned that at one time I saw death in an actual form. He was shown as the "last enemy." I not only saw "death," but he came to me, and laid his hands on me. This is as clearly as I can explain what happened. We all know what we mean when we say "The Lord laid His hands on me." Just so did death. I was in the Spirit at the time, waiting on the Lord. I was looking for the Lord of Life; instead, the messenger of death came. As he put his hands on me, I felt a gradual cessation of the life-flow in my body. It seemed to be put into reverse, so to speak. My blood grew cold, and so did my entire body. The word dissolution went through me. As the life flowed out, the soul and the spirit clung together and began to withdraw gradually from the body. I believe that at this time I experienced that which does really occur at death. This was so real that I have no doubt that had God not intervened, I should actually have died at that time. I was utterly helpless as I lay in my bed. But I remember that in the depths of my soul I said to the Father, "Dear Father what do I do now? You see, after all, death has come, and has put his hands on me. Should I resist him or submit? I confess I don't know what to do. Jesus was obedient to Thy will, even unto death. Thy will be done." At first, there was no answer, and I felt the icy flow of death gradually approaching my heart.

Suddenly, in a loud voice, the Holy Spirit, addressing death personally, cried in me, "The Lord Jesus Christ conquered you upon the cross of Calvary. He tasted death for every man, by the grace of God. You cannot take your prey. The Law of the Spirit of Life in Christ Jesus hath freed this one from the Law of Sin and of Death. Body, soul and spirit, she is redeemed by the Blood of God's Son. Now is brought to pass the saying which is written, 'Death is swallowed up in Victory. Where, O death, is thy sting; where, O grave, is thy victory.'" Then I was moved to finish this Word: "Thanks be unto God which giveth *me* the victory through my Lord Jesus Christ."

However for many days, I was faint and ill, and I know beyond a doubt that the Lord was so gracious as to permit me to taste, ever so slightly, of death. Thus I am very conscious of *body, soul* and *spirit*. In my experiences of rapture, the soul accompanies the spirit on its flight. The body's forces are largely suspended. It may turn very cold, or at times feel "stony." At other times it is just relaxed as in sleep. It still breathes, but is insensible to pain, discomfort, heat or cold. It seems that a slight thread or wire connects the soul and spirit to the body, so that at times the body actually "tugs" at the line, attempting to draw the soul and spirit back, if the rapture is prolonged.

THE WAY INTO RAPTURE

I found that the way into the rapture state varied. At first I felt complete weakness of body and a suspension of my mind—which is normally active and strong. But, in severe illness, the mind was dazed and weak. The sweetest rapture I have experienced is the "swoon of love," In this, as the Bridegroom draws near and reveals Himself, the soul—already "sick of love," as Song of Solomon 2:5 depicts—now actually faints or swoons at His approach. It is ravished in divine love. It loses consciousness of everything, including itself. It flows or flames or throbs with the love of the Heavenly Spouse. It seems to disappear into Him, as a river is lost in the sea. It is not able to comprehend or explain in any natural terms this divine union. The effects of this rapture linger for days. In fact, they are permanent beyond any doubt. Coming out of this state, the mind and heart seem to be left with the Loved One. Others have tasted this rapture and have described it in similar terms. However, the union of love between Christ and each individual soul is absolutely unique. Truly, as the song says, "The joys we share as we tarry there, *none other has ever known.*"

After these times, for days I could think of nothing but Christ. I seemed permeated with His perfume, dripping with divine love which fell upon everyone I encountered. My admiration and love for Him, and the revelation of His interior nature, was such that I could not bear to think or speak of anything save Him. These times of union do change us, for thus *beholding Him we are changed into the same image from glory to glory!*

Another type of rapture occurred when I was suddenly set on my feet by the Spirit and whirled as in a "whirlwind" around and around. I caught a glimpse of Elijah's whirlwind, and at length my body fell prone, but my soul and spirit went up in the whirlwind even to the Throne. It was then that I saw the "Living Creatures," and "Elders."

There is another type we might call flight. In this the soul and spirit seem to flutter in the breast like a bird seeking release. Then, suddenly, they burst out and mount up like a bird in the air. Sometimes this is so sudden that the body faints. There is another type of rapture which begins with singing praise in the Spirit. As I sing I seem to begin to rise, each step of song takes me higher. I am climbing the golden stairs, singing each step of the way, like the priests who paused on each step of the Temple to sing a psalm on feast days. This rapture is always attended by profound revelation.

I want to make it clear that the imagination plays no part in these revelations, nor does the mind reason or question. It is really suspended. The *heart* seems to be the recipient of these revelations. The "eyes" of the heart are opened to divine mysteries. The things I have seen and heard and experienced I had never known previously, with a few exceptions. Nor does the reading of God's Word reveal these mysteries, unless one has been given the key which unlocks them. They have been sealed until the time of the end.

For my part, I have found that under ordinary anointings of the Spirit, the imagination and reasoning faculties still operate. After years of demonstrations, operations and various gift workings, I find that in most cases, at least, the other faculties are still active. Thus, in the midst of deep manifestations, a certain part of my mind is acting like a *sentinel,* checking everything that I say or do with the written Word, watching against error. That this is true is evident, for in many we observe that their own mind and imagination does enter into their manifestation of the Spirit. Thus, the *anointing* may be real; but their *interpretation* of it can be according to their own mind.

James Maloney

In this way error arises, which can be discerned by another. However, in true rapture, all mental faculties are suspended, save those of the New Creation Mind, which is Christ's mind. We may see and hear and learn in amazing clarity the heavenly truths and recall them in minute detail. Oh the wonderful renewing of the mind which takes place, as rapture progresses!

APOCALYPSE

Out of the east I behold Him arise,
Sweeping through the everlasting portal!
Lift up your heads, O golden gates,
He arises, the King Immortal!
His wings, tipped with living fire,
Are outspread from earth to heaven.
His right arm is outstretched in power,
And the stars in His hand are seven!

His feet glow like burnished brass;
His eyes flash with love's pure flames;
And His hair, as white as snowy wool,
His radiant countenance frames.
He is the first and the last,
The Alpha and Omega, the Aleph and the Tau—
Which is, which was, and which is to come
The Almighty whom Daniel saw!

His voice, like the sound of many waters,
Swells to a great deafening roar;
Heaven and earth are all atremble
And are moved as in the days of yore,
When He descended unto Israel

And the heavens themselves were bowed
When His footsteps shook the wilderness
As He marched before His hosts in a cloud!

He that hath eyes, let him watch and see!
He that hath ears, let him hearken and hear!
In the midst of the golden candlesticks He walks,
For this is His hour to appear.
Unto His messengers He speaks,
And His tongue is like a two-edged sword!
O Living Church of the Living God,
Hear the Living Word of the Lord!

—F.M.

THE BIBLE IN THE HEAVENS

Frances Metcalfe

When God created the sun, the moon and the stars He said, "Let there be lights in the firmament of the heaven to divide the day from the night; and let them before signs and for seasons, and for days, and years." (Gen. 1:14) We are all familiar with the seasons, the days, the nights and years as they come and go, and we know that they are governed by the heavenly bodies. But God also said that they are to be SIGNS. A sign is something arbitrarily selected and appointed to represent some other thing. Thus when God said of the celestial luminaries, "and let them be for signs" He meant they should be used to signify something beyond and additional to what they express in their nature and natural offices. The intent of the physical universe is to declare and display the majesty and glory of the Creator. Note the Apostolic assertion, "The invisible things of Him from the creation of the world are clearly seen, being understood by the things that are made, even His eternal power and Godhead." (Rom. 1:20)

Somewhere in the earliest ages of human existence the stars were named and arranged into groups or pictures by someone thoroughly familiar with the great facts of astronomy. Those names and groupings were at the same time included in certain figures natural or imaginary but intensely symbolic and significant. These names and figures have been perpetuated in all the astronomic records of all ages and nations since. They are founded on astronomic truth and form the groundwork of all maps and definitions of the celestial presentations. They are in all the planispheres, celestial globes and star charts among all people from one end of the earth to the other.

These signs and figures are known as the signs of the Zodiac. The scriptural key to these signs is found in one of the most ancient books in the Bible. Job was familiar with the signs and constellations and in writing the book that bears his name he refers to "Mazzaroth." (Job 38:32) "Canst thou bring forth Mazzaroth in his season?" *Young's Analytical Concordance* of the Bible interprets this word as the Twelve Constellations of the Zodiac.

Since the Psalmist affirms that "The heavens declare the glory of God" (Ps. 19:1), are we not then to infer that the story of Christ and redemption is somehow expressed by the stars? David may or may not have so understood it, but the Holy Spirit speaking through him knew the implications of the words. And as it is certain that God meant and ordained the use of heavenly bodies for signs, there would seem to be ample Scriptural warrant for believing that by special divine order and appointment God has written the Gospel in the stars, as well as in the Bible, and that this Gospel, like much of the Sacred Scriptures, is pictorial. "He telleth the number of the stars; He calleth them all by their names." (Ps. 147:4)

The constellations or pictures formed by the stars in primeval astronomy number 48. These are divided into 12 main signs of the Zodiac and their decans or "sidepieces." The Bible in the Heavens is divided into three books of four chapters each. An outline of these books and their chapter headings follows:

BOOK 1—THE REDEEMER

(The First Advent of Jesus Christ)

Chapter 1, The Promise of a Redeemer:

"Behold, a virgin shall conceive, and bear a son, and shall call His name Immanuel." (Isaiah 7:14)

VIRGO

(The Virgin bearing a branch in her right hand and a spike of corn in her left hand): Promised Seed of the woman.

1. COMA (A young mother and child.) The desire of all nations.

2. CENTAURUS (The centaur, half man, half horse, with two natures; holding a spear piercing a victim.) The despised sin offering.

3. BOOTES (Arcturus, the great Shepherd and Harvester, holding a rod and sickle, and walking forth before His flocks.) He cometh.

Chapter 2, The Atoning Work of the Redeemer:

"And they sing a new song, saying, 'Thou art worthy... for Thou wast slain, and hast redeemed us to God by Thy Blood.'" (Revelation 5:9)

LIBRA

(The scales.) The price deficient balanced by the price which covers.

1. CRUX or CROSS (The Cross over which Centaur is advancing, called the Southern Cross.)

2. LUPUS or VICTIMA (Victim of Centaur, slain, pierced to death.) Victory.

3. CORONA or CROWN (The crown which the serpent aims to take, called the Northern Crown), Bestowed.

Chapter 3, The Conflict of the Redeemer:

"Thou shalt tread upon the lion and adder: the young lion and the dragon shalt Thou trample under feet." (Psalm 91:13)

SCORPIO

(The Scorpion seeking to wound, but itself trodden under foot.)

1. SERPENS or SERPENT (The Serpent struggling with the Man, Ophiuchus, desirous of usurping the crown.)

2. OPHIUCHUS (Ophiuchus wrestling with the Serpent, stung in one heel by the Scorpion, and crushing it with the other.) The struggle with the enemy.

3. HERCULES (The Strong One wounded in his heel, kneeling on one knee, humbled in the conflict, the other foot over the Dragon's head, holding in one hand the Golden Apples and the three-headed dog of hell, and in the other the uplifted club.) The mighty Vanquisher.

Chapter 4, The Triumph of the Redeemer—The Triumphant Warrior.

"And in Thy majesty ride prosperously, because of truth and meekness and righteousness; and Thy right hand shall teach Thee terrible things. Thine arrows are sharp in the heart of the King's enemies." (Psalm 45:45)

SAGITTARIUS

(The Archer.) The two-natured Conqueror going forth "Conquering and to conquer."

1. LYRA (An Eagle holding the Harp, as in triumphant gladness.) Praise prepared for the Conqueror.

2. ARA (The Altar, with consuming fires, burning downward, pointing toward Tartarus, prepared for His enemies.) Eternal death.

3. DRACO (The Dragon, the Old Serpent, the Devil, winding himself about the pole in horrid links and contortions.) The enemy cast down from heaven.

BOOK 2—THE REDEEMED

(The Result of the Sufferings of Jesus Christ)

Chapter 1, The Blessings Procured.

"Verily, verily I say unto you, except a corn of wheat fall into the ground and die, it abideth alone: but if it die, it bringeth forth much fruit." (John 12:24)

CAPRICORNUS

(The Fish or Seagoat.) The Goat of Atonement slain for the redeemed.

1. SAGITTA (The arrow.) The arrow of God sent forth. The naked shaft of death.

2. AQUILA (The Eagle.) The smitten One, pierced and falling.

3. DELPHINUS (The Dolphin.) The dead One rising again.

Chapter 2, The Assurance of Blessings.

"If any man thirst, let him come to Me, and drink." (John 7:37)

AQUARIUS

(The water carrier.) The living waters of blessing poured forth for the redeemed.

1. PISCIS AUSTRALIS (The Southern Fish, drinking in the stream.) The blessings bestowed.

2. PEGASUS (The Winged White Horse, speeding as with glad tidings.) The blessings quickly coming.

3. CYGNUS (The Swan on the wing, going and returning, bearing the sign of the Cross.) The Blesser surely returning.

Chapter 3, The Abeyance of Blessings.

"And He said unto them, 'Cast the net on the right side of the ship, and ye shall find.' They cast therefore, and now they were not able to draw it for the multitude of fishes." (John 21:6)

PISCES (The fishes.) The redeemed blessed though bound.

1. THE BAND (Holding up the fishes, and held by the Lamb, it's doubled and fast to the neck of Cetus, binding their great enemy, the sea monster.)

2. ANDROMEDA (The chained woman.) The redeemed in their bondages and affliction.

3. CEPHEUS (The crowned King holding a band and sceptre with his foot planted on the pole star as the great Victor and Lord.) Their Redeemer coming to rule.

Chapter 4, The Consummation of Blessings.

"Worthy is the Lamb that was slain to receive power, and riches, and wisdom, and strength, and honor, and glory, and blessing." (Revelation 5:12)

ARIES

(The Ram or Lamb.) The Lamb that was slain, prepared for victory.

1. CASSIOPEIA (The enthroned Woman.) The captive delivered, preparing for her Husband, the Redeemer.

2. CETUS (The sea-monster.) The great Enemy bound by the Lamb.

3. PERSEUS (The Breaker, an armed man with winged feet, carrying away in triumph the cutoff head of a monster full of writhing serpents, and holding aloft a great sword in his right hand.) Delivering His Redeemed.

BOOK 3—THE REDEEMER

(The Second Advent of Jesus Christ)

Chapter 1. The Coming Messiah King of Kings—The Day of the Lord.

"My horn shall Thou exalt like the horn of an unicorn." (Psalm 92:10)

TAURUS

(The Bull.) Messiah corning to rule.

1. ORION (The glorious, brilliant Prince, with a sword girded on his side, and his foot on the head of the Serpent.) Light breaking forth in the person of the Redeemer.

2. ERIDANUS (The tortuous river of the Judge.) The wrath of God.

3. AURIGA (The Shepherd.) Safety in the day of that wrath.

Chapter 2, (The Twins) The Twofold Nature of the King.

1. LEPUS (The Hare, or Serpent.) The enemy trodden under foot.

2. CANIS MAJOR (The great dog, or Sirius.) The glorious Prince.

3. CANIS MINOR (The second dog, or Procyon.) The exalted Redeemer.

Chapter 3, The Redemption of Messiah's Possession.

"I will multiply thy seed... and thy seed shall possess the gate of his enemies." (Genesis 22:17)

CANCER

(The crab.) The possessions held fast.

1. URSA MINOR (The lesser bear. Anciently the lesser sheepfold.)

2. URSA MAJOR (The greater bear. Anciently the greater sheepfold, in connection with Arcturus, the guardian of the flock.)

3. ARGO (The Ship.) The company of travellers under the bright Canopus, their Prince. The Redeemed pilgrims safe at home.

Chapter 4, The Glorious Triumph of the Messiah—The Consummated Victory.

"Weep not: behold the Lion of the tribe of Judah, the root of David, hath prevailed to open the book and to loose the seven seals thereof." (Revelation 5:5)

LEO

(The Lion.) The Lion of the Tribe of Judah aroused for the rending of the enemy.

1. HYDRA (The fleeing serpent.) That old serpent, the Devil, trodden under foot by the crab and lion.

2. CRATER (Cup) The cup of Divine wrath poured out upon the serpent.

3. CORVUS (The crow or raven.) The birds of prey and doom tearing the serpent and devouring him and his followers.

GOD'S TIME AND
THE BIBLE CALENDAR

Frances Metcalfe

GOD'S TIME AND THE BIBLE CALENDAR was originally published in multigraphed form by Frances Metcalfe and The Golden Candlestick fellowship in 1941. Each year we sent out a new calendar, giving the current Biblical dates. However, it is not difficult to calculate the beginning of each Biblical month by utilizing a Gregorian calendar, that gives the dates of the New Moon, and using the instructions in this booklet.

Recently and unexpectedly, the Holy Spirit impressed us to have it printed, and we believe that it will be of special interest to you who are aware of, and are attuned to, His times and seasons. During the past few months we have had an unusual number of requests for this writing, which is mentioned in THE FEASTS OF THE SEVENTH MONTH booklet.

"You know what a critical hour this is, how it is *high time* for you to wake up out of your sleep rouse to reality. For salvation (final deliverance) is nearer to us now than when we first believed. The night is far gone the day is almost here. Let us then drop (fling away) the works and deeds of darkness and put on the (full) armor of light... Let us live and conduct ourselves honorably (as befitting sons of God) as in the open light of day." (Romans 13:11, 12, 14 Amplified)

—Marian Pickard

GOD'S TIME

God has a time for everything
And for every purpose beneath the sun;
He has a perfect schedule
By which the universe is run.

The stars vary not in their courses,
The sun's cycles do not deviate;
And God relentlessly pursues His path,
Never too early, never too late.

It is an irrefutable fact that God has His own set times and seasons for accomplishing His purposes and fulfilling His Word. Century after century, God's plan for man has been unfolding in perfect accord with His appointed times—God's time is as immutable as His Word! It is equally certain that the Bible should and does reveal God's own unique calendar which He established "in the beginning." Nevertheless, few men have accurate knowledge of this calendar; nor do they possess understanding concerning His appointed times. Instead of following the Bible calendar, they live by the altered and corrupted time-schedules devised by man. So throughout the world we find many different calendars, not one of which is in perfect accord with God's time. This is not to be wondered at, for Satan has always sought to confuse men concerning God's Word and His times. One of the marks of the AntiChrist is that "he shall think to change times and laws." (Daniel 7:25) Even among "the saints of the Most High God" there is little enlightenment about this subject. Because of ignorance they do not become attuned to His rhythm, nor do they detect the ticking and striking of His unerring clock.

In the days of the Patriarchs such knowledge and attunement did exist. They understood that God was running the earth on a heaven-set stellar chronometer. Had not God said: "Let there be lights in the firmament of the heaven to divide the day from the night; and let them be for *signs,* and for *seasons,* and for *days,* and *years!*" The knowledge of the meaning of the stars, both as to signs and seasons, and the ability to tell time by the great star-clock, which God had placed in the northern sky, was handed down from father to son. But, gradually, through disobedience and sin, men lost count of God's time and became disoriented from it.

However, this did not prevent His time-pattern from continuing to unfold as His clock ticked out the centuries. When, at His appointed time (faithfully predicted and pre-figured in His Word) God brought Israel forth out of the land of Egypt, He revealed to them His calendar and seasons and His seven sacred feasts. They faithfully observed His sacred day (the sabbath), and His week, month and year. Later on, as their love grew cold and they became disobedient, they also grew indifferent to these things. And, when they departed from Him; they followed the profane calendars of the pagan nations wherein they dwelt. It is highly significant that *in every period of restoration they again observed the Bible Calendar.*

"Why, seeing times are not hidden from the Almighty, are those who know Him ignorant of His days?" (Job 24:1; Literal Translation)

A wise and righteous man asked this question many centuries ago. The Holy Spirit is asking this pertinent question again today. Why is it that so many Christians are ignorant about God's time and calendar? Even among Bible students this ignorance exists. And why is it that so few are interested in the subject? We hear many talking about the signs of the times, but of what use is it to observe the *signs* if we do not know the *times?* Are they—and we—not repeating the mistake of those who failed to recognize God's fullness of time for the coming of His Son into the world? Their scholars had studied the Messianic Scriptures for generations, yet they knew not the hour of their visitation. In fact, Israel was noted for almost *never* knowing God's times for manifestation! And there is a similar blindness today. Behind us lie centuries of the open Bible. It is widely read and taught; yet few Christians understand God's plan for "the time of the end." Nor do they realize that even now we are in the midst of the apocalyptic appearing of Jesus Christ to His prepared ones—an appearing which takes place secretly—before His great worldwide manifestation as Judge and King. It is evident that God's Word is more or less a closed book unless the blessed Holy Spirit reveals and interprets it to the heart of the believer. It is He who breaks the seals of the Word on earth, just as it is the Lamb who breaks the seals in Heaven! Praise God for the wonderful Teacher He has sent to guide us into all truth! It is of *His revelation concerning God's Time that we write.* We had no knowledge of the matter whatsoever, until He undertook to instruct us. That which He has revealed to us—and to others with whom He has joined us—we gladly share with you. We do so as *witnesses,* and believe that as you read this testimony, He, the true Teacher, will add His own precious witness to it and will confirm it to your hearts.

Our beloved Paul taught us that we are "stewards of the mysteries of God," and that it is required of stewards that they be found faithful. (1 Cor. 4:1, 2) "God's Time" is one of these mysteries, and we want to prove faithful in the stewardship of whatever light He has imparted to us concerning it. We want to make it clear at the outset that we had no previous knowledge or conception of it, nor were we interested in obtaining such. Chronologies seemed tiresome and, as for prophetic date-setting—well, such a thing seemed both confusing and unscriptural as far as we could see. We were of the opinion that it was not for us to know times and seasons, and that such knowledge was vested in the Father alone. Therefore, it came as a real surprise when the Holy Spirit first began to deal with us about God's time. And this was no recent thing, we assure you, for it began in December, 1941.

For a number of years prior to this time we had been conscious of God's Plan for "the time of the end," and had been in preparation for it. But we had no light about the actual time for its accomplishment, beyond the strong impression that it was near at hand. Then, one night I had a vivid dream-vision, and in the vision a Heavenly being talked with me about "the winding up of the age." He showed me a large scroll, and on it were written the major events and the dates on which they would occur. As I studied it, a great joy and light flooded my being! I was filled with praise and rejoicing, as though all things were already accomplished. I saw that they had been pre-determined from the beginning, and that they would soon be openly manifested. I marvelled that I could know and understand just *when* each glorious happening would take place. It was all so simple. No need to puzzle about prophecies now—I knew! The glory of this visitation lasted most of the night. I awoke with a new sense of expectancy and assurance—the Kingdom seemed so close! I wanted to write all the dates down at once, so I would not forget them; but when I went to do so, I discovered that I could not recall even one of them! Try as I would, I could not recall them. I felt dismayed and sought the Lord in prayer. He confirmed the reality of the vision, but made it clear to me that He was not going to restore the dates to my conscious mind. They would remain in my subconscious, however, and I would have a new insight about His timing. He showed me that He wanted us to fully realize that great events are just at hand, and that it is important for us to be "timed" with Him in every move.

During the early part of 1942, the Holy Spirit continued to impress upon me about time. Various Scriptures would come to me over and over. I had little idea of their hidden meaning. So I would pray and wait on the Lord concerning each one, asking Him to enlighten me. One of the first that came was:

"To everything there is a *season,* and a *time* for every purpose under heaven... God hath made everything beautiful in HIS time... Who is the wise man? And who knoweth the interpretation of a thing?... A wise man's (or woman's) heart discerneth both time and judgment." (Ecc. 3:1, 11; 8:1, 5)

The Spirit seemed to whisper in my heart something like this: "You have listened to Me as I have taught you about My judgments, and you believe that they are now in the earth. You have given yourself to me for prayer and intercession, dedicating yourself to Me for My endtime purposes, as I have asked. This is good! But now I would have you to learn also of My *times,* for the days are at hand for the fulfillment of prophecy, and *the set time to favor Zion has come.*" These last words rang over and over in my heart. At times He would ask a simple question: "What time is it?" At first I took it literally and would tell Him the time by my watch. Then He would seem a little amused and would say, "Yes, you are able to tell time by man's clock; but what do you know of time according to My clock?" And I would say, "Lord, I do not know Your times; I cannot see Your clock, so please teach me." Another portion of the Word that came again and again was the entire third chapter of Ecclesiastes, and I saw that it had a spiritual as well as a literal meaning.

I also learned that Jesus was very conscious of time. He made many references to it and was always aware of the Father's time. I saw that Paul and Peter also referred often to it. Other portions of Scripture that came to my mind were:

"And that, *knowing the time* that now it is *high time* to awake out of sleep; for now is our salvation nearer than when we believed." (Romans 13:11)

"He hath determined the times before appointed." (Acts 17:26)

"Until the *appearing* of our Lord Jesus Christ which *in His times* He shall show... " (1 Timothy 6:15)

One day the Lord spoke to me clearly in this word: "Of the times and seasons, I would not have you be ignorant." I supposed this was a quotation from Scripture, but the nearest I could find to it were the words of Paul:

"But of the times and the seasons, brethren, ye have no need that I write unto you. For yourselves *know perfectly...* " (1 Thess. 5:1)

As I read this, the Holy Ghost came upon me in a blessed way. He made it plain that those early Christians to whom Paul wrote did indeed know God's times and seasons, for they were taught and led by the Holy Spirit. There was no need that any day should come upon them unawares, for they were enlightened—"the children of the day." And this same word was meant to apply to us. The words of our Lord, as recorded in Acts 1:7 also came to me:

"It is not for you to know the times or the seasons, which the Father hath put in His own power."

But I saw that He spoke these words to the disciples *before* they had received the enduement of the Holy Spirit. After He came upon them, He taught them "all things, yea, the deep things of God." I put myself in His hands in a definite way and called upon Him to reveal God's times and seasons, promising Him that I would cherish such knowledge and would seek always to be timed with Him in his movings.

From then on the Holy Spirit dealt with me as though I had enrolled for a special course of study. I know you will understand exactly what I mean by this, for many of you have had similar experiences. The wonderful School of the Holy Spirit offers many courses for our edification. From subject to subject—as well as from glory to glory—we are led. How blessed are those of whom it can be said:

"The anointing which ye have received of Him abideth in you, and ye need not that any man teach you; but as the same anointing teacheth you of all things, and is truth, and is no lie, and even as it hath taught you, ye shall abide in Him." (1 John 2:27)

I soon discovered that the Lord was speaking about God's Time to others who were close to me in the Spirit, and they were as surprised and previously uninformed about it as I. At this point I would like to make it clear that at no time did the Spirit's dealing assume a *legalistic* quality. Nor did the knowledge of God's Calendar, which He imparted to us, become a matter of working out our salvation by the observance of certain days or outward forms. I realize that some of the Lord's people *do* feel such compunctions, and I am sure that each of us should obey his own conscience toward God in these matters, as well as all others. However, in our case, the Spirit placed the emphasis upon the *spiritual* meaning of His calendar, and upon the *prophetic* significance of its events. We relied entirely upon the grace of God in Christ Jesus for our salvation then, just as we do today. And our interest in His Sabbaths and feasts was not like that of those to whom Paul referred in Galatians 4:10. We found a wonderful source of joy and enlightenment in these dealings, and never, in any sense of the word, was there a tendency to stress the letter of the Word, rather than the Spirit of it. During the years that have intervened between that time and the present, the Lord has consistently continued to unfold the truths He revealed to us then. Furthermore, He has caused these things to be confirmed through many other witnesses. In our little company of The Golden Candlestick He has moved in harmony with His appointed times and seasons, year after year. And it has been a pleasure to us to be timed by His clock, and to observe His calendar, His seasons and His feasts.

Now, to turn our attention back to the events of early 1942. One night as a sister and I spent several hours together in prayer, the presence of the Lord was unusually manifested. After a time, a holy awe silenced us before Him, and as we waited, not knowing just what to expect, I heard these words as though spoken in the depths of my heart: "I must keep the Passover with you." I was familiar with the term Passover, and immediately associated it with Moses and the Old Testament. So, of course, I was puzzled as to what the Lord meant. As I continued to wait upon Him, I had an inner vision of Jesus and His disciples as they gathered together in the Upper Room for the Last Supper. And it was made clear to me that we were to observe it in some similar way—and in an upper room! I was also given to understand that I was not to invite anyone to this Supper, but that the Lord would be the Host and would summon each one whom He desired to be present. Five more words were impressed upon my heart: "Set your house in order." I continued to wait upon the Lord, and a solemnity I had never felt before settled upon my spirit. Then, just before I arose from my knees, He said: "Forty days are appointed."

The other sister had been silent and worshipful too, and for a few minutes we felt restrained from saying a word. Then, timidly, she queried, "Frances, have you ever heard of Christians keeping the Passover? I seem to feel that the Lord wants us to keep it this year." I hesitated, wondering if I were free to tell her of my own impressions. We had been accustomed to being disciplined concerning speaking of the things the Spirit had entrusted to us, waiting always for His leading. In this instance it came immediately, so I told her what I had seen and heard, and we agreed that we would speak of it to no one else, but wait for Him to do so in His own time and way. As soon as I got home I got out a calendar and counted out forty days, and *it ended on the very night of Passover.* But I did not know enough about Bible dates to realize it at the time, so I concluded that the meaning of the forty days was that I was to set my house in order and spend much time in prayer during that period.

A few days later, another friend called me and said that she too had received a strange Scripture: "With desire have I desired to eat this Passover with you." (Luke 22:15) The Holy Spirit filled us with rejoicing! Another one had been bidden! The next one who spoke to me was a brother who had worshiped with us from time to time. He too had been summoned. And we all took it very seriously, spending all the time we could in prayer, and seeking to be cleansed of everything that might offend the Lord. When the forty days were nearing an end, we all began to become a little anxious, for we did not know *where* nor exactly *when* we were to gather. We knew, of course, that we could not set the date for the Passover according to our own planning. For many years we had been taught to be timed with God as far as individual obedience was concerned, and we had also learned to let the Spirit set the times and places of our meetings, as He led us to "break bread from house to house." So we had no will of our own about the time to keep the Passover, but neither did we know God's will about it. Then one day it dawned upon us that the Bible would reveal the correct date. Surely enough, there in Exodus 12, we found it—the evening of the fourteenth day of the month Abib. But we still didn't know how to determine when the Bible month began, nor how it fitted in with our Gregorian calendar. So we searched a little further, and it was this very thing that started the wheels of our "chronometer" turning in harmony with God's infallible time.

First of all, we learned that God had established His own Sacred New Year at the time when He brought Israel out of Egypt, and that He has never abrogated it. We found out that it begins each year at the time of the new moon which occurs nearest to the vernal equinox—Springtime! Man may overlook the date, but nature remembers it and celebrates it each year by adorning the face of the earth with resurrection glory. The bird-choir with its myriad voices proclaims God's season of new birth, and paeans His praise!

After we knew the date of the first of Abib, it was a simple matter to count to the 14th day, and thus establish our Passover time. This date was the day after the end of the forty days of which the Spirit had spoken. It was a relief to know the date. But we still did not know the location of the "upper room." Our faith was somewhat tested about this, for the Lord made no move until only three days were left before the 14th of Abib. Then He moved fast! To tell you how He provided that upper room would be a long story in itself, so I can merely sketch it.

A sister, who knew nothing whatever about our Passover plans, contacted us and invited us for a prayer meeting. I asked her, "Does your house have an upper room?" "O, yes," she said, "a large one, just perfect for a prayer room, and I have dedicated it to God for that purpose." We immediately began to rejoice, and the Spirit bore witness that this was indeed His chosen "upper room."

Several of us helped prepare it for the long-awaited Passover; and, in some ways, we felt as rushed as the Israelites did when they hastened out of Egypt on that first Passover night.

Thirteen of us were present in the upper room upon that occasion, and not one of us will ever forget that holy and memorable night. I will not attempt to describe in this writing the wonderful manifestation of the presence of the Lord, nor to relate the new and awesome ways in which the Spirit moved in our midst. This would require many pages. Truly, that night was a night of "beginnings" for us, the open door into a sabbatical year of glory during which our Lord Jesus appeared to us again and again.

As we prepared to leave the upper room, long after midnight, the Lord revealed that we were return on the night of the 16th of Abib, at which time He would again manifest His power and glory. We did not know that the 16th would be the Bible time for the offering of the Omer, or first sheaf (Firstfruits.) Nor were we prepared for what He had in store for us. We learned later that most interpreters of the Bible agree that this type (Leviticus 23:10-12) refers to the resurrection of Jesus from the grave, and His ascension, and that it further typifies the translation and the glorification of all believers at the time of His second coming.

We gathered, expecting it to be another very solemn gathering; but, instead, a glorious spirit of praise fell upon us, and for hours we sang and rejoiced in the Spirit! Then, in a very unique way, the Spirit depicted the Marriage Supper of the Lamb, and gave us a little foretaste of the inexpressible joy that will be the portion of those who shall partake of it. He also gave us a vivid and unforgettable picture of the sorrow and torment of those who find the door shut and are left in the outer darkness. Another unforgettable night! The Holy Spirit engraved the Word of God upon our hearts in an ineffaceable way. Without our realizing it, the Spirit had thus commemorated the first two of the Seven Sacred Feasts of Jehovah. These auspicious "feasts" were the beginning of a "sabbatical year" for us, and during the year all the Seven Feasts in their proper order were renewed in our midst. The Spirit almost invariably assembled us at the time of the new moon or full moon or the seventh day of the week. The Bible pattern of time unfolded month after month.

We have related the beginning of our revelation of God's Time in considerable detail, in order that it may be clear that the dealing was entirely of the Holy Spirit, and not the outgrowth of anyone's ideas or interpretations. We would enjoy also telling you the rest of that wonderful experience, but you can readily see that we must condense the balance for the sake of expediency.

Low in the west hangs the silvery new moon,
Heralding the dawn of God's new year.
Silence leans down from the distant stars
To lift our praise up swiftly to His ear.

Our planet earth is bathed in darkness, now—
No ray of light, except the mystic flame
That burns within our hearts as we invoke
The sacred power, immortal fire, of Jesus' name.

—M.P.

GOD'S GREAT CLOCK

One of the questions heard most frequently in our modern world is, "What time is it?" And no one presumes to ignore the all-important factor of time. It is not necessary to point out that every phase of our daily life is run on this basis, and that without it our entire social and economic structure would be turned into confusion. We all agree that time is valuable, and we are displeased with anyone who robs us of time by being tardy in regard to working for us or keeping an appointment with us. Within each of our breasts God has placed a unique little clock whose ticking, or more properly, beating, continually reminds us that our lives are counting off their allotted minutes and hours—that time is running out. When our heart-clock stops, mortal life ends for us. Scientists agree that the human heart is one of the most delicate and amazing mechanisms known to man. This type of clock, which God has placed in each one of His creatures is but a tiny miniature of the great clock which God "wound up" and placed in the northern heavens when He created the firmament. Century after century it has counted off God's years with immutable accuracy, slowly marking off the time God has alloted to mankind.

In order to understand the meaning of the master Time Schedule designed by God, we must first see that He has a great plan for the human race, and that this plan is to be fully accomplished within an appointed time. It is thrilling to know that the very days in which we are privileged to live are known as "The Time of the End," and that the last portion of the time is running out. This knowledge ought to cause us to rejoice and to know that it is indeed "high time to awaken out of slumber." In Isaiah 45:18, we find a lucid statement of God's original purpose for man: "For thus saith the Lord that created the heavens; God Himself that formed the earth and made it; He hath established it, He created it *not in vain, He formed it to be inhabited."* Reading on, we learn that His main purpose for the inhabitants of this world is that they were to be His *worshipers.* "Who hath declared this from ancient time? Who hath told it from that time? Have not I the Lord? There is no God beside Me... Look unto Me and be ye saved all the ends of the earth..."

Since it is impossible for sinful men to be true worshipers of God, the plan of salvation was designed before the creation of the world— for God had foreknowledge that man would sin. *Worship,* then, was the first purpose; *Salvation,* the secondary. As we have mentioned, God has appointed a period of time during which the plan of salvation is in operation. And, to date, every step of that plan has been carried out exactly according to the schedule! It will continue to be in operation until the great angel declares its fulfillment and its end. (Rev. 10:5, 6) One of these days, *time shall be no more!*

In the very first chapter of Genesis, God reveals His pattern of time. The first unit mentioned is a *day.* Now a day may refer to a twelve hour day, such as Jesus spoke of in John 11:9, or it may mean a thousand years. (2 Peter 3:8) But, here in Genesis, He makes it plain that He is defining a *day* as twelve hours, or the hours in which there is light as contrasted with night. In John 11:9, Jesus said, "Are there not twelve hours in a day?" "God's day" begins not with the rising sun, but with its setting: "And the evening and the morning were the first day." Of course we know that a day represents the time required for the earth to make one complete turn on its axis. We now count our days from midnight to midnight. The pagans usually counted theirs from sunrise to sunrise, for most of them were sun worshipers. But God's covenant people began their day when the sun had set—a prophetical pre-showing of how the Holy Seed will begin their new day when man's sun has set and the earth's day is ended!

The second unit of time mentioned in Genesis is that of a *week.* Ordinarily, a week refers to seven days; but it may indicate seven years, or, as it is the case with man's allotted time, it may be composed of seven thousand-year days. Most Bible students are agreed that six thousand years will have elapsed between Adam and the beginning of the millenium. Man's week of work shall thus end with God's great Sabbath. However, the Bible year is found to be composed of 360 days, and not 365¼ days, such as our present Gregorian year. This discrepancy is a confusing thing, and it is difficult to explain. Some suppose that in the beginning the earth did complete its orbit around the sun in 360 days, instead of the 365¼ days it now requires. They also believe that in the beginning the earth was not tipped on its axis as it is now. Of course, if the earth was not tipped there would be no variation in the length of the days, and the days and nights would be of the same length every day of the year. There would be no seasons, such as we now have, for it is this 23½ degree tilt of the axis, as we know, that produces the progression of seasons. The Holy Spirit did not tell us just how it came to be so, but He did make it plain that some cataclysmic event threw the earth off its axis. And He confirmed God's year-length as being 360 days. (The great pyramid reveals many things concerning God's time cycles and in it is found the 360 day measurement, as well as that of 365¼ days.) It is this difference in measurement that makes the computation of long-range time periods so difficult. God's 6,000 years will therefore be shorter than man's! ("Except the time be shortened... ") (Matt. 24:22)

The "cataclysmic event" might well have been the Noahic Flood. Some believe that the uneven distribution of water caused its weight to accumulate in one place and thus to tilt the earth on its axis. It may be very significant that God's covenant of the seasons is first spoken of immediately after the flood. (Genesis 8:22) Thus the rainbow is considered a symbol of *time,* as well as of *promise.* Man has never been able to devise a perfect calendar which adjusts to earth's altered cycles. Even the Gregorian calendar has to add an additional day every four years—and then it is not exact. The Jewish calendar still follows the 360-day schedule. To compensate for the remaining time, they add an intercalary month every three years, and make other alterations from time to time.

The next unit mentioned in the Bible is the *month.* (Genesis 7:11) God's month begins with the appearance of the new moon and lasts until the four phases of the moon have run their course. (He has likewise ordered the physiological processes in woman's body in this cycle, and made natural birth a type of the second birth and regeneration.) It is a most significant fact that we are now told by psychologists and physicians that the moon has as definite an effect upon the minds and emotions of man as it does upon the tides of the sea and the cycles of plant growth. At new moon and at full moon strong emotional and inspirational forces play upon the human soul. Many poets wrote their finest poems at such times. Lovers have always found the moon their ally. Musicians, artists, writers—yes, men in every walk of life will admit that the moon has a definite effect upon them. The Lord called His people to *worship* at new moon and at full moon. He turned their eyes away from the comparatively small and insignificant sun of our solar system, and caused them to look and see the millions of greater suns that light up the universe. He caused them to lift up their hearts into the Living God and rise on the tide of pure emotion and worship into His Presence.

It would be a simple thing to adopt the present Jewish calendar and assume that we were thus adjusting ourselves to the Bible calendar. But it too has been altered, and scholars agree that it has been so confused that none really knows what year it is. The present year of the Jewish calendar is 5739 (after the creation.) But Bible experts say that Bible chronologies were not computed correctly and that it is much later than this. Our Gregorian year is 1979. Allowing for four thousand years from Adam to Christ (the usually accepted period), we would therefore be in the year 5979. But this too is erroneous! We know that it has been proved that Jesus was born from three to five years earlier than is indicated by our calendar. In order to find the true calendar then, we must search for it in the Bible and seek understanding of it from the Holy Spirit. There is no way to be positive of the *year* in which we are living, but it is possible to know God's appointed months, weeks, days and seasons. And it is gratifying to find that when we do make this effort to follow His times, the Holy Spirit assists us to move in such harmony with the Word that the Bible becomes like a new book.

If you want to find God's great clock in the northern sky it is not difficult to do so. And when you once learn the position of the stars, you can tell time within a few minutes, by observing their relation to one another. All time moves in cycles or circles. The rotation of the earth producing the day, as we have mentioned, the revolving of the moon around the earth gives us the month, and the revolution of the earth around the sun produces the year. The sun itself whirls around some distant center, carrying its planets with it. Man's instruments for telling time are circular in form—clocks, watches, chronometers. God's instrument is circular also. He has placed in the northern skies a pole star, often called Polaris, and it is the center of the dial of His great clock. A radius extending 40 degrees in every direction from the North Star marks the outer rim of the crystal, and the Big Dipper forms the hour-hand. This hour-hand makes one complete circle around the face of this star-clock in exactly 24 hours, never varying a second. (Sun time does vary.) It marks the yearly cycle just as accurately. Our chronometers are set by this star-clock. (The Dipper, the Seven Stars: Amos 5:8.) Man used to use sundials, hour glasses, and other crude means of telling time; but today even the poorest man may possess a watch which can be set to perfect time each day. Oh, that man's heart and spirit might be as easily adjusted to God's heavenly time! Solomon rejoiced that

God had given him not only wisdom but knowledge. Included in this knowledge was perfect knowledge about God's times.

"For it is He that has given me the unerring knowledge of what is, to know the constitution of the world and the working of the elements; the beginning and end and middle periods of time, the alternations of solstices and the changes of the seasons, the cycles of the years and the positions of the stars." (Wisdom of Solomon 7:17-19; Apocrypha)

David cried out, "My times are in Thy hand!" And how often have we cried out these very words to God; and with what comfort we have rested in Him, knowing that our days and weeks and months and years are all in his keeping. Yes, *our times* are in His hand. How wonderful it would be if *His times* were established in *our hearts!*

—Frances Metcalfe

CHRIST CUT TIME IN TWO

When the fulness of time was come
God sent forth His son.
So it was written and so it was done!
At the time of Incarnation
And manifest Salvation,
God came to earth in flesh,
Emmanuel! The Holy One!

This was the time that ended time,
That cut time in two
Between the old and the new.
Thy coming, Lord,
Fulfilled and ended all that had been
And was the beginning of all that will ever be.
B.C.—A.D.! B.C.—A.D.!

And Thy birth, Thy coming in us, Lord,
Cut *our* time in two—
Between the old nature and the new!
We count our time A.D. not B.C.
We are in the new time, the new way,
The New Covenant—Praises be!

—F.M.

THE BIBLE CALENDAR

"We should have the moon for our calendar." (Psalm 104:19; Knox)

The original Bible calendar is based on the lunar month—the length of time required for the moon to make its orbit around the earth. Almost all other calendars, including our Gregorian, are based upon the solar year—the time required for the earth to complete its orbit about the sun. To compensate for the discrepancy between lunar and solar time, an intercalary month has been added to the Bible calendar approximately every three years.

The Bible New Year begins in the spring, at the new moon which appears nearest to the time of the vernal equinox. This time was appointed unto Israel by the Word of the Lord when He brought them forth out of Egypt. Also, please notice that the dates for the Feasts were set, and were to be celebrated accordingly: "These are the feasts of the LORD, even Holy Convocations which ye shall proclaim in their seasons." (Lev. 23:4) Before the Exodus, Israel observed their New Year in the fall—the supposed time of the Creation. Nature keeps her New Year in accordance with God's—in the springtime! Until the 17th century, our Gregorian calendar also started in the spring.

The present Jewish calendar—which is patterned on the Bible Calendar—observes the fall date. Their civil year begins in the fall. However, they also observe the "Sacred New Year" in the spring for certain religious purposes. Their calendar differs from the Biblical pattern in several ways, having been altered during the time of the Babylonian captivity, both as to certain times and the names of the months. They also adjust holy days so as not to conflict with weekly sabbaths. Our dates are based on the Scriptural pattern in the Old Testament. The New Testament dates are not recorded in the Bible. So these included have been taken from the research of eminent

Bible scholars. They are controversial, but we have included them as a matter of interest. This Jewish year, which began last September, is 5739. But this date is admitted to be possibly erroneous.

These are the names of the months and dates on which each new moon occurs in 1979. The first day of the month is the day following the new moon.

January 28-Shebat	July 24-Av
February 26-Adar	August 22-Elul
March 28-Abib	September 21-Tishri
April26-Iyar	October 20-Chesvan
May 26-Sivan	November 19-Kislev
June 24-Tammuz	December 19-Tebet

THE FIRST MONTH—ABIB

Abib means "green fruit" or "young ear." After the Babylonian captivity, the Jews renamed this month to Nisan, meaning "month of flowers." This is the time that the spring or latter rains occur in the Holy Land, and when the barley harvest begins. It typifies deliverance, redemption, rebirth, resurrection, "latter rain," blessing and harvest.

Abib 1—NEW YEAR'S DAY—Holy Convocation (Ex. 12)

Abib 10—Preparation for Passover begins

Abib 14—PASSOVER—Full moon (Ex. 12; Lev. 23; Deut. 16)

Abib 15—The beginning of Feast of Unleavened Bread (7 days—Ex. 13:4-10)

Abib 16—Offering of Omer (Firstfruits). The beginning of the Feast of Weeks. (Lev. 23:10-14)

Abib 21—Holy Convocation. End of the Feast of Unleavened Bread.

Important events which occurred during the month.

Abib 1—The tabernacle of the tent of the congregation was set up in the wilderness. (One year after the exodus. Ex. 40:1,2)

Abib 10—Joshua led the people through the Jordan. (40 years after the exodus. Joshua 4:19)

Abib 14—Josiah reestablished the Passover. (2 Chron. 29:15-36)

Abib 14—The children of the captivity kept the Passover with joy. (Ezra 6:19-22)

Abib 24—Daniel beheld the wonderful vision of the Lord. (Daniel 10:4-21)

During this month the Children of Israel entered the Wilderness of Zin, and Moses smote the rock which brought forth water. (Num. 20:7-13)

Our Lord was also smitten during this month, and both blood and water flowed from His riven side. This month is forever sacred to the Christian, for it was during this season that Jesus endured His great sufferings and was crucified for our sins. It is the month of the Resurrection as well—and of the beginning of His forty days of post resurrection appearing on earth. The exact dates of these events are disputed by the Bible scholars, but of one thing we may be sure, God's timing is exact and, since all these events were prefigured in the Old Testament, they are certain to have occurred on the dates which the types occurred.

Jesus was crucified on the exact Passover date. He kept the Passover with His disciples and then established the TRUE PASSOVER—of which the other was only a type—THE LORD'S SUPPER. He died on the exact day and the exact hour of the slaying of the Passover Lamb.

In our modern times many visitations of the Lord have occurred during this sacred month. It is said that "The Azusa Street Outpouring" in Los Angeles began on the night of Passover (1906.) Many other outpourings have taken place during this season, in various places. The entire Christian world is drawn very close to our Lord during these weeks. And it is not surprising that it should be a time of special revival and blessing the world over.

Our Resurrection date is now computed by the moon. It occurs on the first Sunday after the first full moon following the vernal equinox. However, prior to 325 A.D., the Resurrection was celebrated at Passover. At the Council of Nicaea it was decided to set aside a Sunday and to make it uniform the world over. Jesus was crucified on the true Biblical Passover. The Jews kept theirs one day later, as they do today.

THE SECOND MONTH—ZIF

This name signifies brightness and splendor. The Jews call this month by the Babylonian name, Iyyar. It is at this season that the earth seems to be in full flowering. In the Holy Land the barley harvest reaches its fulness. Most of the "rains are over and gone" and "the time of the singing of birds has come," indeed.

Zif 1—NEW MOON—HOLY CONVOCATION

Zif 10—The supposed time of Elijah's translation. Jews keep a fast in his memory.

Zif 14—The second or "little" Passover (designed for those who had missed Passover—Num. 9:9-11)

Zif 27—Ascension Day—40 days after offering of Omer.

Zif 28—Supposed time of the death of Samuel. (Jews keep a fast.)

Important events which occurred during this month.

Zif 1—The Lord numbered the Children of Israel the second year after they came out of Egypt. (Num, 1:1-18)

Zif 2—Solomon began the construction of the temple. (1 Kings 6:37; 2 Chron. 3:2)

Zif 14—Hezekiah summoned Israel and Judah to keep the Passover, since they had not been prepared to keep it during the first month. (2 Chron. 30:2, 13, 15)

Zif 15—The Children of Israel came to the Wilderness of Sin and murmured there before the Lord. God sent them the manna. (Ex. 16:1)

During this month Zerubbabel and Joshua laid the foundation of the Temple, accompanied by trumpets and praise and shouting. (Ezra 3) This month seems to typify harvesting (spring), building and increase.

It was during this month that our Lord appeared on earth after His resurrection. In the history of the Church, it is recorded that century after century this season has often been blessed by unusual manifestations of God's presence and glory.

THE THIRD MONTH—SIVAN

The meaning of Sivan is "glorious," and this third month is indeed a time of fulfillment and glory. It is the time of the early wheat harvest in Palestine. The rain and thunder clouds disappear, and heavy dews descend. (Psalms 133:3; Hosea 14:5)

Sivan 1—NEW MOON—HOLY CONVOCATION

Sivan 6—End of the Feast of Weeks (Lev. 23)

Sivan 7—PENTECOST (50th day) (Lev. 23; Deut. 16:9; Acts 2:15-22)

Important events which occurred during this month.

The Children of Israel arrived at Sinai and camped before the Mount of God. Moses went up into the Mount to receive the Ten Commandments. (The prefiguring of the outpouring of the Spirit and the birth of the Church at Pentecost.)

Asa heard the word of the prophet and abolished idolatry in all the land of Judah and Benjamin. In the third month he gathered the people together in Jerusalem and they made a great offering unto the Lord, renewing their covenant with Him. (2 Chron. 15:8-15)

In the days of Queen Esther, it was during this month that the decree reversing the order against the Jews was issued. Letters were dispatched to the rulers of one hundred twenty-seven provinces, freeing them from the cruel order conceived by Haman. (Esther 8:9)

The third month was the season of the birth of the Church. It is a Covenant Month, a time of consecration and heavenly visitation. Israel came to the Mount—the Church to the "Upper Room." Who knows what other great events may occur at this "set time to favor Zion"?

THE FOURTH MONTH—TAMMUZ

The original Hebrew name for this month seems to have been lost. Tarnmuz is Babylonian in origin and refers to a heathen concept of a god called "the son of life." It falls in the hot, dry summer season in the Holy Land—the time of the first-ripe figs and early vintage. The Bible records very little about this month.

Tammuz 1—NEW MOON—HOLY CONVOCATION

Tammuz 17—The Jews observed a fast to commemorate the breach in the wall of Jerusalem. (Jer. 52:5-7)

This month seems to have been a rather dry and trying time in Israel. In the early days of the church the believers suffered much persecution and were sent forth at this season—immediately following Pentecost—bearing the Word of Life.

THE FIFTH MONTH—AB

Also called AV. It means "God as Father." This month is the season of intense heat in Palestine. For the Jews it is a somewhat ominous month, sometimes referred to as the month of doom or judgment.

Ab 1—NEW MOON—HOLY CONVOCATION

Ab 9—The Jews observe a special fast, recalling the destruction of the Temple by Nebuchadnezzar, 586 B.C. (2 Kings 25:8,9)

Important events which occurred during this month.

The ninth of Ab is the most tragic day in the Hebrew calendar, and has long been a day of mourning in Israel. In the last twenty-five hundred years, at least fifteen major calamities have happened to the Jews on this date.

Nebuchadnezzar began his attack on this day. He took away the best of the Jews into captivity. On this same day in 70 A.D. the bitterest calamity of Jewish history befell them: Jerusalem was destroyed again, this time by the Roman Emperor Titus. (The fulfillment of Jesus' prophecy.) The Jewish people ceased to exist as a nation. In the next century another slaughter took place on this date on the plains of Megiddo—where Hadrian crushed the uprising led by Bar Kochba. A year later the Emperor Trajan plowed under the site of Jerusalem, destroying all evidence that there had been a Jewish state. This too happened on the ninth of Ab. Many other attacks against the Jews took place on this date in various nations. Even in modem times this date has come into play, for it was on this day the Arabs began their attacks upon Jews at the Wailing Wall in Jerusalem in 1929. It is no wonder that the Jews call this day, "Armageddon Day."

THE SIXTH MONTH—ELUL

The sixth month falls at the time of the beginning of the autumn harvest season in Palestine. Its meaning is "to reap." This month is also called, "the beginning of the days of awe," and is a special preparatory time in which Israel seeks the Lord and begins to look ahead to the glorious seventh month of harvest and rejoicing. In some places the shofar is still sounded every day as a reminder of the "high and holy days" to come.

Elul 1—NEW MOON—HOLY CONVOCATION.

Elul 7—The Jews celebrate the dedication of the walls of Jerusalem which were completed at this time. (Neh. 12)

Important events which occurred during this month.

On the fifth day of this month the Lord spoke to Zerubbabel and Joshua, through Haggai, concerning the building of the "latter house." And on the 24th day of the month He stirred up the remnant of the people to give themselves to the work of the House of the Lord. (Hag. 1) On the fifth day of the sixth month, the Lord appeared unto Ezekiel in great glory. (Ezek. 8:1)

THE SEVENTH MONTH—TISHRI

It was also called Ethanim, meaning "permanent streams." This month is the high time of all the year. The former or early rains fall in Palestine, and the harvest is gathered in. The fruits are fully ripened, and the songs of the vintage ring far and near.

The month dawns with great solemnity. All Israel is called to attention with the blowing of trumpets. After the awesome days pass, comes the time of rejoicing, the most glorious time of all the year!

Tishri 1—NEW MOON—THE FEAST OF TRUMPETS. This is the Jewish New Year—Rosh Hashanah. (Lev. 23, 24; Num. 29:1) Followed by nine days of fasting, prayer and repentance.

Tishri 10—THE GREAT DAY OF ATONEMENT—YOM KIPPUR (Lev. 23:26-32)

Tishri 15—Beginning of the FEAST OF TABERNACLES (Lev. 23:34-44)

Tishri 23—The Great Day of the Feast (John 7:37, 38; Lev. 23:39)

Important events which occurred during this month.

Until the time of the Exodus, this month was considered to be the first month of the year—the supposed time of the creation of the earth. Joseph is said to have been released from his Egyptian prison on the tenth day of Tishri.

Solomon dedicated the Temple during this season. And, instead of keeping the Feast of Tabernacles for eight days only, kept it for another week—making fifteen full days. The Ark of the Covenant was set in place and great rejoicing and praise was manifest. The Shekinah glory of God filled the Temple. (1 Kings 8:2; 2 Chron. 5:3)

In the days of restoration Ezra and Nehemiah led the people in keeping the feasts. (Ezra 3; Nehemiah 8:2-17)

Ezekiel prophesied that this feast would be observed in the Kingdom Age, perhaps as a memorial. (Ezek. 45:25; See also Zech. 14:16-21)

It was on the twenty-first day of this month that Haggai received the prophecy concerning the glory of the latter house. (Haggai 2:1)

Year after year this season has been a time of special visitation and blessing in our midst. The Spirit is speaking to many today concerning the latter day antitype of the "Feast of Tabernacles" and the "Harvest of Ingathering." (See our writing, "The Feasts of the Seventh Month.")

THE EIGHTH MONTH—BUL

Bul means "ram." It is also called Chesvan which is Babylonian and means "floods." In Palestine the rains are unusually heavy at this season. The ground is prepared for the sowing of the spring harvest.

Bul 1—NEW MOON—HOLY CONVOCATION. No other Bible dates are recorded for this month.

Important events which occurred during this month.

It is believed that Noah entered the Ark on the tenth of Bul. And on the seventeenth the windows of heaven were opened. (Gen. 7)

Solomon's Temple was completed during this month. (1 Kings 6:38)

Zechariah received his vision concerning Jerusalem at this season. (Zech. 1:1)

Although little is said in our Bible about the Eighth month Feast, it is referred to in various Apocryphal writings. The Holy Spirit has led us to sanctify this month in a special way, for it was by His direction that on the first day of the 8th month the first issue of the Golden Candlestick was put into the mail in 1943. Our star is the eight-pointed star. And 8 in Scripture is the resurrection, recreation number. We have been directed to rejoice in this month and honor Zion, the Jerusalem from Above, the True Church, the Bride of the Lamb.

THE NINTH MONTH—KISLEV

The meaning of this name is hard to trace. This month is the beginning of winter in Palestine.

Kislev 1—NEW MOON—HOLY CONVOCATION

Kislev 25—FEAST OF DEDICATION—Hanukkah, or the Festival of Lights. (Jno. 10:22, 23; 1 Maccabees 4:52-61, Apocrypha) This continues for eight days.

Important events which occurred during this month.

Ezra gathered and exhorted the people on the 20th day of this month. (Ezra 10:9)

A fast was proclaimed and Baruch read the Word of the Lord to the Congregation. (Jeremiah 36:9,10)

Rededication, cleansing and devotion to the Word of the Lord seem to characterize this month. (See also Nehemiah 1:1; Zech. 7:1.)

Jesus visited Jerusalem at this Feast. (John 10:22, 23)

THE TENTH MONTH—TEBET

The meaning of this month is obscure. Little of importance is recorded concerning it. The mountain regions of Palestine are cold and snowy, while the first wild flowers begin to appear in the plains.

Tebet 1—NEW MOON—HOLY CONVOCATION

Tebet 2—End of Hanukkah.

Important events which occurred during this month.

It was at this time that Esther was brought unto the King—her marriage month, and the time of her crowning. (Esther 2:16)

THE ELEVENTH MONTH—SHEBAT

One meaning for Shebat is "a rod." This month marks the beginning of spring in Palestine.

Shebat 1—NEW MOON—HOLY CONVOCATION

(For references of interest, see Deut. 1:3; 1; Chron. 27:14; Zech. 1:7.)

THE TWELFTH MONTH—ADAR

The meaning of the month is "fire." It is the beginning of the budding of the trees in Palestine. And the citrus fruits are ripe in the. lowlands.

Adar 1—NEW MOON—HOLY CONVOCATION

Adar 13—The fast of Esther (Esther 4)

Adar 14, 15—The Feast of Purim (Esther 9)

(See also 2 Kings 25:27; 1 Chron. 27:15; Jer. 52:31; Ezek 32:1; 2 Macc. 15:36.)

THE FEASTS OF THE SEVENTH MONTH

Frances Metcalfe

"Behold upon the mountains the feet of him that bringeth
good tidings, that publisheth peace! O Judah, keep thy
solemn feasts, perform thy vows." (Nahum 1:15)

INTRODUCTION

T he sacred yearly feasts of Israel were three: Passover, Pentecost and Tabernacles. (Lev. 23) Each of these feasts held great prophetic, as well as historic, significance. Though they were initiated in the Old Testament, under the dispensation of the Covenant of the Law, it is in the New Testament, and during the dispensation of the Grace Covenant, that they find their fulfillment. In addition to these three major feasts, there were four additional accompanying feasts—bringing the total to seven. These are: The Feast of Unleavened Bread (typifying communion with Christ in a holy walk), The Feast of Firstfruits (signifying the resurrection of Christ), The Feast of Trumpets (foreshadowing the regathering of Israel and the beginning of a new age), and The Day of Atonement (the repentance and redemption of all Israel.) (Lev. 23; Deut. 16) These feasts were established by the direct command of JHVH (I Am that I Am), when He delivered Israel out of the land of Egypt. They are called "set feasts" because they continue the same, as to time and manner of observance, year after year, generation after generation. Through His servant, Moses, the Lord established them as ordinances to be observed forever.

The significance and importance of the feasts cannot be confined to the land in which they began, nor to the people with whom they were instituted. They do not find their consummation under the Old Covenant of the Law. As glorious as these beginnings must have been, there is a far greater glory to be manifested in their fulfillment in the New Covenant. We have already seen the greater Passover at Calvary and the greater Pentecost in the Upper Room. However, the fulfillment of the *Feast of Tabernacles* and the feasts which accompany it—called the Feasts of the Seventh Month—has not yet taken place. The Harvest of Ingathering comes at the *end* of the age. Like all prophecy, these feasts have a spiritual as well as literal fulfillment, and they will continue even in the kingdom Age, according to the prophecies of Ezekiel and Zechariah, when they will be celebrated by the entire world—as a memorial, no doubt. (Ezek. 45:18-25; 46:9,10; Zech. 14:16-18)

Before continuing, we might mention that there were other feasts also observed under the Old Testament dispensation. But these were not instituted as perpetual feasts by the Lord. Among those still celebrated by the Jews is the Feast of Purim, based upon the book of Esther. (This feast too has a prophetic significance, of course, for the Church, the Bride of Christ, of which Esther is a type.) Thus, in Adar (usually in our month of March), on the 14th and 15th days, Esther's sacrifice, courage, faith and victory for her people are commemorated in various ways. The Feast of Dedication, which occurs in December, near Christmas, is even more widely celebrated by the Jews. Now called Hanukkah, or the Festival of Lights, it is used to represent civil, as well as religious, liberty, and continues for eight days. The origin of this feast is found in 1 Maccabees 4:52-61, Apocrypha. That the Lord Jesus Christ attended this feast, at least upon one occasion, is recorded in John 10:22,23.

We all know that the Lord's dealings with Israel, under the Law, are shadows and types of greater things to come. The book of

Hebrews reveals that the Tabernacle and the ordinances of worship, under the Old Covenant, present a perfect picture of the plan of redemption—which was fulfilled in the person of Jesus Christ, our great High Priest. The account of the wilderness wanderings of the holy people of God is preserved for us, that we might be admonished and warned of the dangers of unbelief and disobedience. Paul tells us: "Now all these things happened unto them for ensamples (types), and they are written for our admonition, upon whom the ends of the world (age) are come." (1 Cor. 10: 11)

Since the outpouring of the Holy Spirit in these latter days, there is a growing interest in the types and anti-types of the Old Testament. The Spirit-taught, Spirit-led saints find that He illuminates these things to them in a surprising and glorious way. This is especially true of those who have entered into the Kingdom as little children and have learned how to cherish the mysteries of the Kingdom. "I thank Thee, O Father, Lord of heaven and earth, because Thou hast hid these things from the wise and prudent, and hast revealed them unto babes." (Matt. 11:25) Even now they enjoy foretastes of the Kingdom of God on earth. They know that the Davidic Covenant has been renewed, the Kingdom line reestablished, and that even now our King is ruling through His Zion-people by the power of the Spirit. (Zech. 12: 8; Acts 15:16) The Kingdom will not remain hidden much longer! Praise God, soon it will be manifested openly! "Fear not, little flock; for it is your Father's good pleasure to give you the Kingdom." (Luke 12:32) Especially to the "little flock" is the writing about the Feasts of the Seventh Month dedicated.

When the natural seasons come,
At whatever time may be;
When too the months begin;
On their feasts and on holy days,
As they come in order due,
Each as a memorial in its season,
I shall hold it as one of the laws
Engraven of old on the tablets,
To render to God as my tribute—
The blessings of my lips.
When the natural years begin;
At the turning-points of their seasons,
And when each completes its term
On its natural day,
Yielding each to each—
Reaping time to summer;
Sowing time to verdure;
I shall hold it as one of the laws
Engraven of old on the tablets,
To offer to God as my fruits—
The praises of my tongue
And to cull for Him as my tithe—
The skilled music of my lips.

—Part of a hymn from The Dead Sea Scrolls

FOREWORD

We of the Golden Candlestick Fellowship have enjoyed a most remarkable renewing of the Sacred Feasts of the Lord in our midst, beginning in 1942. The Holy Spirit Himself was our sole teacher and guide, for we had no previous knowledge either of Jehovah's feasts or of the Bible calendar. Since we were living in the glorious freedom of the Grace Covenant, we had mentally relegated the Old Testament feasts to the past. And we were totally ignorant of God's own calendar, which He established in the beginning. But when the blessed Holy Spirit stirred our hearts to renew the Sacred Feasts—not under the Law, but in newness of life, by the Spirit—we had much joy in obeying Him, for He made it clear that in doing so we would be glorifying the Lord and His Word, linking the worship of the Old Testament with the glorious worship of the New Testament. Following our High Priest beyond the veil, we likewise would participate in demonstrating the fulfillment of Leviticus 23, through Jesus Christ and His anointed ones, according to the teaching of the Book of Hebrews.

It may be of interest to you to know that this year, 1972, the date of the Feast of Trumpets and Jewish New Year is September 8. The Great Day of Atonement, Yom Kippur, occurs on September 18. And the Feast of Tabernacles begins on September 23. For those of you who have a special interest in the Bible calendar, we have prepared a writing called GOD'S TIME AND BIBLE CALENDAR. These will be sent upon request, as long as our supply lasts.

—Frances Metcalfe

WHEN THE SACRED SEVENTH MONTH IS DRAWING NEAR

When the sacred seventh month is drawing near,
Then hearts begin to stir in Israel;

113

For "the high and holy days" will soon be here,
And what may happen, who can tell?
In Israel, God's Israel,
What may happen, who can tell?

It seems the heavens are brooding just above,
And angels are as near to us as men;
Diffusing everywhere our Father's love,
And attuning us to praise the Lord again.
In Israel, God's Israel,
Attuning us to praise the Lord again.

So we'll gather as before to keep Jehovah's feasts,
According to His everlasting Word.
Oh, may our faith and fervor be increased
To praise and magnify the Living Lord.
In Israel, God's Israel,
We praise and magnify the Living Lord.

—F.M.

"Blessed—happy, fortunate (to be envied)—are the people who know the joyful sound (who understand and appreciate the spiritual blessings symbolized by the feasts); they walk, O Lord, in the light and favor of Your countenance!" (Psalm 89:15; Amplified)

THE ORIGIN AND MEANING OF THE FEAST

In order to understand the Feast of Tabernacles—the major feast of the seventh month—and the other feasts which accompany it, it will be helpful to trace the origin of the word itself and to discover its exact meaning. When we speak of a feast, we are prone to picture a banquet of rich foods and an evening of entertainment. But such is not the original concept of the word. Festival comes a little nearer to expressing the thought. It suggests gala attire, parades, singing, dancing—a holiday spent in celebrating some new event or in commemorating one in the past. Yet this word falls short also, so let us examine it in the Bible text.

The Hebrew word translated feast is *chag*. It refers to a *sacred* feast—not an ordinary meal given for entertainment. Its original meaning is a procession, a dance, or a public dramatization of some event. The eating and drinking which accompanied it were of secondary importance. From the earliest times it was the custom of heathen peoples to observe certain festal days. Primarily these seasons were for the purpose of worshiping or appeasing their idols or gods. The occasion gave them an opportunity to openly display their beliefs, by various forms of art and ceremony, and thus to instruct all who witnessed the celebration in the tenets of their religion. This custom continues to this very day among primitive peoples. Our own American Indians, though now educated according to our way of life, still preserve their cultural and religious heritage by the means of such ceremonies and festivals.

We must remember that in Old Testament times they had no books or other means of teaching one another. Most of the religions confined their ordinances to a small body of priests, and the common man had little or no religious instruction. As for the women and children, they were excluded almost entirely. However, the feast was the exception to this rule. When the festal season dawned, all work and business were laid aside, and old and young alike donned their finest garments and jewels and joined the great crowds in an open display of "worship." The main events of the festivity took place in the streets or at their heathen temples, where the history or meaning of the particular occasion was depicted on banners and other signs and decorations. It was sung and demonstrated in the dance and drama, and typified by the various foods which were selected for refreshment. As the feast increased in fervor, the people drank more and more wine and worked themselves up into a frantic zeal and excitement. The practices accompanying the pagan feasts were as vile as the nature of the gods they served. So licentious did they become toward the climax of their festivities that they openly displayed their shameful practices in the public streets. Because of these things, the Hebrews never participated in them. Their teachers forbade them to look upon any object of heathen worship. During their sojourn in Egypt, no doubt some of them learned to tolerate the frequent Egyptian revels; but for the most part they remained aloof.

There is no authentic indication that the Israelites ever celebrated ceremonial feasts until the time of their deliverance from Egypt. It is a matter of profound significance that their feasting began with their deliverance, and that the idea of it did not originate in their own hearts. They abhorred such affairs! No, it was formed in the heart of JHVH Himself! He desired to take His people into the wilderness, that they might worship Him and keep a feast with Him. He made known His wish through His servant Moses: "And Moses said, We will go with our young and with our old, with our sons and with our daughters, with our flocks and with our herds will we go; for we must hold a *feast* unto the LORD." (Ex. 10:9)

How wonderful to discover that we have a God who hungers, thirsts, deeply desires, to feast with His people—a God who from the beginning has tried to show us that His greatest delight is not in showing His authority, but in enjoying the close fellowship of His children. It is true that He disciplines, that He asks for sacrifice, fasting, travail and tears—in their proper place. But He turns the sacrifice into rejoicing, the ashes into beauty, the fast into a feast! He set a feast of fruits before Adam and Eve, the like of which man has never been able to reproduce, and He communed with them face to face. He ate with Abraham in his tent at noonday. He spread a table in the wilderness for the entire nation of His chosen, and gave them the very bread of heaven. Jesus performed His first miracle at a wedding feast. He fed five thousand on a hillside. He did not hesitate to attend feasts, nor to eat with publicans and sinners. He also attended the Feast of Dedication and the Feast of Tabernacles (John 7:37; 10:22) during His three years of public ministry. He heartily desired to keep the Passover with His inner circle, and on that occasion He established the New Covenant with a Feast, wherein He gave the redeemed His own Body for their meat and His own Blood for their drink, in symbolic form. He has promised through the prophet Isaiah that in the latter days He will make a feast, a great feast for all nations, upon His Holy Mount. (Isaiah 25:6) And the greatest feast of all—the marriage supper of the Lamb—will usher in the new age of His reign in glory. (Rev. 19:9)

Yes, we have a God who delights in the feast, whether we understand this part of His nature or not. He wants to be worshiped in the beauty of holiness, and—at times—in beautiful array (vestments of joy.) He gave the arts to man to be used for His worship, and He finds great pleasure in the sacred dance, drama, song, and in every expression of beauty known to the human heart. *Through David He made known His delight in such praise by causing him to set apart four thousand Levites, out of twenty-eight thousand, to do nothing but praise, sing and play on instruments, and rehearse His mighty acts.* (1 Chron. 23:5; 2 Chron. 29:25-28)

"Blessed are the people who know the joyful sound!" (Psalm 89: 15) But this rejoicing must be a holy rejoicing, exceedingly solemn as well as joyful. It is not to become a time of self-indulgence, such as the heathen made of their festivals. When Israel kept only the form and ceremony of the feasts, and lost the holiness and true spirit of them in revelings, they were rebuked by the Lord; even as St. Paul rebuked the Corinthians who turned the early Agape feasts of the Church into a time of drunkenness and gluttony. But the Lord never abolished the feasts, and we dare say that He never will. The old song says, "With Jesus we shall feast eternally." And our hearts say a hearty "Amen!"

"I, Ezra, received a command from the Lord on Mount Horeb, to go to Israel: but when I went to them, they refused me and rejected the Lord's command. Therefore I say unto you, heathen, who hear and understand, expect your shepherd; He will give you everlasting rest, for He is close at hand, who will come at the end of the world. *Be ready for the rewards of the Kingdom,* for everlasting light will shine upon you forever. Flee from the shadow of this world, receive the enjoyment of your glory. I call my Savior to witness publicly. *Receive the approval of the Lord and rejoice with thanksgiving to Him who has called you to heavenly realms.*

"Get up and stand and see the number of those *who are marked with His seal at the feast of the Lord.* Those who have removed from the shadow of the world have received splendid garments from the Lord. Receive your number, Zion, and close the list of your people who are clothed in white who have fulfilled the law of the Lord... Entreat the Lord's power that your people may be made holy." (2 Esdras 2:31-41)

THE SACRED CALENDAR

Not only did the Lord reveal Himself unto Israel in the ordinances of Tabernacle worship and in the sacred feasts, but also in the ordinances of the heavens—the sun, moon, and stars, and in the changing seasons of the year. (Gen. 1:14) Israel's calendar was different from those of the heathen nations round about them. Man's ways are not God's ways, nor is man's time God's time. The heathen set their time by the sun, and they worshiped the sun in one way or another. But God ordered Israel to set their time by the moon and to count the day from the sun's setting, rather than its rising. In Genesis 1 we read again and again: "And the evening and the morning were the first day... the second day... the third day... " God began His day at sundown and His people were commanded to do likewise. We shall have to shift our reckoning from the solar year to the lunar year in order to understand God's timing. Psalm 104:19 says: "He appointed the moon for seasons." The Knox version here is emphatic: "We should have the moon for our calendar."

Since the lunar month is shorter than the solar month, and the seasons follow the latter, it became necessary for the Hebrews to add an intercalary month—a 13th month—once every three years. The sacred new year begins at the new moon which occurs *nearest* to the Vernal Equinox (the equinox is on March 21-22 on our calendar.) It was at this time that the Lord brought Israel out of Egypt. "And the Lord spake unto Moses... This month shall be unto you the beginning of months: it shall be the first month of the year to you." (Ex. 12:1,2) Evidently up until this time they had reckoned time from what is now called the civil new year, which occurs in the fall. This is the supposed time of the creation of the world. We must bear in mind that to this very day the Jewish calendar has two "new years"—one in the spring, the sacred year, and one in the fall, the civil year.

When we speak of the Feasts of the Seventh Month we refer to the sacred year which begins at the new moon in the month Abib or Nisan. The seventh month is called Tishri (meaning to open) and also Ethanim (permanent streams.) It is likewise the first month of the civil year. This month occurs during the latter part of September or the early part of October in our calendar. Sometimes the appearing of the new moon at Jerusalem may vary a day. The Jews take their time from there, of course.

The number "seven" was the Lord's covenant number with Israel. God rested upon the seventh day at the time of the creation recorded in Genesis, and He hallowed this day. His people observed it as a Sabbath. The number seven always carried with it a sacred significance. The Feast of Weeks, which followed Passover, was kept for seven weeks—the fiftieth day being Pentecost. Likewise the seventh month was considered the high and holy time of the year. Its principle feast—Tabernacles (Succoth)—is referred to as the "Great Feast." This was the most glorious time of all the year, a time of jubilation and of heavenly visitation. The seventh year was likewise hallowed, becoming a Sabbatical Year, wherein the ground must be given rest—not worked by man.

And seven times seven years led into the fiftieth year—Jubilee! The number seven continues on throughout the Scriptures and appears again in great prominence in the book of The Revelation, where it is used in reference to judgments, trumpets, vials, etc., at which time Israel is again in Covenant relationship with the Lord. The ten tribes will have been regathered and the "two sticks" will be "one" in His hand. (Ezek. 37:16-19) The 144,000 will have been sealed, and all will be in preparation for the New Age.

To all spiritual people this number has come to mean God's number—perfection, fulfillment. There are seven dispensations of time preceding the New Covenant: The Edenic, Adamic, Noahic, Abrahamic, Mosaic, Palestinian and Davidic. The New Covenant number is *eight,* the resurrection, re-creation number. Of the glories of the New Creation and of the New Heavens and the New Earth we cannot now speak, for this writing deals with the fulfillment of the Seventh Month and the seventh dispensation into which the world is soon entering. Nearly six thousand years have passed since the Edenic Covenant. Due to the various changes man has made in regard to calendars, Bible students do not agree as to the exact time, but we all agree, I am sure, that it is time for the *Harvest of Ingathering,* which Jesus said would come at the end of the age, when, from out of every tongue and tribe and nation, the Husbandman shall reap His glorious harvest.

THE HOLY SEVENTH MONTH

It's the holy Seventh Month—
Our God desires a feast!
The golden harvest moon
Is shining in the east.
With eager hearts we come,
For we have waited long
To offer to Jehovah
Our joyful festal song.

To this Tabernacle Feast
We've come from far and near,
To celebrate and tell
The blessings of the year.
With expectations high
And hearts with love aflame,
We've made this pilgrimage
To glorify His Name.

James Maloney

O hear the shofar call—
The silver trumpets sound!
The holy feast begins,
Processions gather 'round!
The singers form a choir
While others wave the palms;
With voices clear and high
We sing the Hallel Psalms.

The consecrated priests
In beautiful attire,
Are burning incense sweet
Upon the altar fire;
Their praise and prayers ascend
With songs in one accord.
And suddenly—we see
The glory of the Lord!

—Eddy Schafer

THE FEAST OF TRUMPETS

(Lev. 23:24; Num. 10:10; 29:1)

Tishri, the seventh month, began with two days of holy convocation. When the new moon appeared, the shofars were blown loud and long. At the beginning of the other months the blasts were shorter and fewer. "Blow ye the trumpet at the new moon, in the time appointed, on our solemn feast day." (Psalm 81:3) The shofar, or ram's horn, has a high, penetrating sound, and when it is blown by an expert it can make a most disturbing and arousing cry. The city of Jerusalem, and all the surrounding territory, could hear these blasts, which were prolonged and frequently repeated. The effect was to sound an alarm, which alerted the people in preparation for the important days at hand. "Blow ye the trumpet in Zion, and sound an alarm in my holy mountain; let all the inhabitants of the land tremble: for the day of the Lord cometh, for it is nigh at hand... Sanctify a fast, call a solemn assembly." (Joel 2:1,15) The Israelites believed that the shofar frightened their enemies and even the devil himself, and they used it frequently in battle. Thus the Feast of Trumpets seems to have a number of purposes: A proclaiming of the day of the Lord; a warning and an alarm to His people; a challenge to His foes; and the sign of an advance!

The civil new year, known as Rosh Hashanah, was celebrated on this day. Most of the day was spent in worship. No work of any kind could be done. Between the first day of Tishri and the Great Day of Atonement, which falls on the 10th day, there were eight days for repentance, fasting and prayer. A sense of impending judgment was felt by all, and there was a solemnity even in the more joyful aspects. When Ezra reestablished this day (Neh. 8) the people stood in the street before the water gate for hours, while he read to them out of the Book of the Law. "And Ezra blessed the LORD, the great

God. And all the people answered, Amen, Amen, with lifting up their hands; and they bowed their heads and worshiped the LORD with their faces toward the ground." (Neh. 8:6) They were so overcome that they wept; then Ezra comforted them with words which have become dear to all of us: "Go your way, eat the fat, and drink the sweet, and send portions unto them for whom nothing is prepared: for this day is holy unto our Lord, neither be ye sorry; for *the joy of the LORD is your strength.*" (Neh. 8:9,10)

Need I try to interpret to you the latter-day fulfillment of this feast? I am sure that we are all aware that the trumpet has been sounding in Zion for some time, and that the Spirit has been arousing and warning God's people on every hand. By means of preaching, reaching, prophecies, demonstrations, inspired writings, songs—yes, by innumerable operations of the Spirit He has made known the beginning of "The Day of the Lord."

THE SACRED SUMMONS

Once again we hear the sacred summons,
His trumpets are ringing loud and clear!
Once again we know that we're included
In the high and holy days of God's year.

Once again we don our festal garments,
After washing in the water of the Word;
And through the Blood we know we shall find access
To the very presence of the Lord.

Once again, as priests, we climb the mountain
Where the altar fires are aflame,
And we gather with a host of saints and angels
To adore and acclaim the Sacred Name!

—Frances Metcalfe

THE GREAT DAY OF ATONEMENT

(Lev. 16; 23:26-32)

During the eight days between the Feast of Trumpets and the great Day of Atonement, the people were occupied with prayer and repentance. The more devout ones fasted and prayed, not only for themselves but for all Israel. Restitution was made with one another, wrongs were righted, and forgiveness sought. Great fear was connected with Atonement Day; all alike believed that unless every requirement of the Lord was met, judgment would be sure and swift to follow. It was the most solemn time of the year, culminating with the Great Day which began at sunset on the ninth day. No food could be eaten until the following evening, and many of the devout prayed and watched all night.

In the meantime, the High Priest had left his own home and had spent this time in the Temple preparing for the sacred duties of the Great Day. This was the only day in the year when he could enter the Holy of Holies. He knew that in order to do so he would have to take his life in his hands, so to speak. When the day finally dawned, the people assembled early in the outer court. Leviticus 16 gives us the detailed picture of the procedure. For a further account of this ceremony we quote from an authentic Jewish historical book:

The High Priest first performs the daily offering in the presence of the people. For this service he is clad in his golden vestments. He washes his hands at the golden basin and proceeds to offer the daily sacrifice. The people stand enthralled at the sight. From their point of observation the High Priest is a glowing spectacle, with his golden miter (on which is written the sacred name, JHVH), the precious gems on his breast, and the golden bells which hang on the hem of his purple robe, and which tinkle with every movement that he makes. He then goes into the anteroom in order to burn the incense upon the golden altar, and to put the lamps of the Menorah (golden candlestick) in order. This ends the daily service; now comes the Yom Kippur service for which the High Priest must bathe and don the white linen garments. When he enters the court again, clad in white, he makes an even stronger impression on the assemblage than when he appeared in gold. The young bull that is destined for the sacrifice stands ready between the porch and the altar. The High Priest lays his hands on the bull's head and makes a confession of sin and appeals for mercy. Three times during this prayer he expressly pronounces the ineffable Name, JHVH, which no Israelite is permitted to speak. He ends with these words, "It is said, 'On this day shall atonement be made for you, to cleanse you; from all your sins shall ye be clean before the Lord.'"

Then follows the ceremony of the sacrificial goats; the scapegoat is led away into the wilderness, the other one is sacrificed. After this second confessional, the bull is slaughtered and his blood gathered in a basin. The High Priest walks up the ramp leading to the altar and fills the censer with burning coals. He takes this with him into the Holy of Holies, and pours the sacred incense upon the coals as he stands before the Mercy-Seat. The Holy of Holies is filled with fragrant smoke, and the presence of the Lord is said to appear in the Cloud above the Ark. All this elaborate and most solemn ceremony is carried on while the people await outside, prostrate and silent before the Lord. Great awe and fear grip every heart. Only when the High Priest at last emerges, clad -again in his glorious garments, do the people rejoice. Then follows a long reading of the Law, during which, at intervals, the people lift their voices and bless God. At the close of the day a special feast is held in each home, and great joy reigns throughout the city. Everyone is lighthearted and filled with expectation of even greater rejoicing which is soon to follow in the celebration of the Feast of Tabernacles.

In the ninth chapter of Hebrews we find the anti-type of Leviticus 16. Our High Priest has entered into the Holy of Holies in the heavens, and has taken His own blood to the eternal Mercy Seat. Not only has He prevailed for the sins of Israel; but for those of everyone born into the world. Our iniquities have not only been *covered,* but *borne away,* as typified by the scapegoat sent into the wilderness. He has fulfilled and done away with the Aaronic priesthood and has established a new priesthood after the order of Melchizedek, which abides forever. The priests of the New Covenant are permitted to follow Him beyond the veil, even into the Holy of Holies, there to intercede for all men. And when our High Priest comes forth out of that Sanctuary and appears again before the world clad in His beautiful garments, then shall come that great manifestation of salvation which is to be consummated at the end of the age. "Unto them that look for Him shall He appear the second time without sin unto salvation." (Heb. 9:28)

There is another sense also in which the Great Day of Atonement has a fulfillment in our own day. For many years the Spirit-led saints have been fasting and praying for a mighty visitation of God in a revival which will bring salvation to multitudes the world over. Many of them have passed through experiences similar to those of the Israelites during their eight days of repentance. The fear of the Lord has gripped them; they have made restitution, and have sought forgiveness for themselves and for all the world, praying that the judgments of God might not fall, beseeching Him that in the midst of wrath He will remember mercy. They have left off ministering to the people and have had a change of garments, so that they might "go beyond the veil" to intercede and to prevail before God. They offer Him the incense of their praise, arising from the flame He has kindled in their hearts. They learn to speak the unutterable Name, and to prevail through the merit of the blood of the Lamb of God, which they offer in the name of Jesus. God appears to them, too, in a "cloud." And they shall know when the hour comes for them to go back to the outer court, clad in glorious garments. The hour for rejoicing shall come! Great salvation is about to be manifested! The Feast of Tabernacles and the Harvest of Ingathering are just ahead!

All the Hosts of Heaven speak the mighty word:
    The Lord is King!
All on earth abiding make the blessing heard:
    The Lord was King of yore!
These and those that soar and praise together chant:
    The Lord shall be King forevermore!
All of Heaven's envoys signal banners raise:
    The Lord is King!
Let all the earth sing songs of praise:
    The Lord was King of yore!
And let all faithful hearts together shout:
    The Lord shall be King forevermore!
All the guardian angels truthfully repeat:
    The Lord is King!
All the throngs assembled make the sound complete:
    The Lord was King of yore!
And the chiefest singers triumph as they sing:
    The Lord shall be King forevermore!
All the stars unnumbered tell the word on high:
    The Lord is King!
All creation joins the stirring cry:
    The Lord was King of yore!
Let all on earth with praise make it known:
    The Lord shall be King forevermore!
                    —from the Hebrew Liturgy for Rosh Hashanah

THE FEAST OF TABERNACLES

(Lev. 23:24-44; Num. 28:10)

The Feast of Tabernacles has several other names: Feast of Booths; Succoth; Harvest of Ingathering; and The Great Feast. It was celebrated at vintage time, when most of the harvest had been gathered in and the people were free to give themselves to unstinted rejoicing. It was imperative for all the heads of families to be in Jerusalem for this feast, and as a rule they were accompanied by other members of their families who were able to attend. It is significant that this feast of exultant praise and joy came immediately after a time of solemnity and fasting. First the fast— then the feast! This was, and is, the order of the Lord. Otherwise their feast of joy might have turned into wild revelings, such as the heathen feasts. JHVH desired His people to feast and to have pleasure in singing and dancing and celebrating their blessings. But this joy was to be an innocent joy, highly spiritual in character, even though expressed in the natural beauties and bounties which He had given them. As one writer has said: "It is well known from olden time that the Baalim of the heathen temples possessed the power to whip the blood of mortal men into a fury of intoxication; while the joy of the Spirit, free from drunkenness and lust, was solely the gift of the God of Jacob." Ezra reminded them of this "joy of the Lord" when he reestablished the feasts, and all the people were given to understand that the Lord was feasting with them.

The day following Atonement was spent in preparing the tabernacles or booths. One of the purposes of the feast was to remind the Israelites of the days when they lived in the wilderness and had no homes, vineyards or orchards. Their harvest might be rich and full now; but there had been a time when they had to be fed by manna from heaven. They were never to forget the wonderful mercies of the Lord which had been shown to them in the wilderness. It was an ordinance that the men must dwell in the booths of branches of trees for seven days, while the women and children partook of meals with them there. They used the branches of the palm (their sacred tree), citron, myrtle, and other trees, to erect these temporary dwellings.

In the meantime, the pilgrims from the countryside began to arrive in caravans. No one came alone to the feast—it was unthinkable! And it is certain that we too must move in fellowship with others as we approach the Holy City. There is no "going it alone" to Zion's Hill, even though the preparatory days were often lonely. What a comfort is this concept of togetherness! Some came from great distances, having arranged to meet with others along the way, so that they might renew their friendship and sing and rejoice together while on pilgrimage. The 84th Psalm gives us a vivid picture of such processions. As they neared the City the crowd increased, and the singing and shouting grew louder. One writer says:

The pilgrims approach the City. From the hilltops the towers and roofs of Jerusalem are visible. They look upon the City and sing: "As the mountains are round about Jerusalem, so the Lord is round about His people from this time forth and forever." As they come nearer they begin the 122nd and 125th Psalms. By this time the Temple is clearly visible to the pilgrims. The golden plates with which it is covered glisten in the sun and the white marble dazzles their eyes; they are silent with awe as they view the house of God, the goal of their journey.

When they reach the outside of the gates, representatives of the City meet them and welcome them; then they select one of their number to be their leader. He then stands up before the caravan and calls out: "Arise ye, and let us go up unto Mount Zion, to the house of the Lord our God!" He starts out and the others follow. The people are in an exalted mood. They are on their way to Zion and they know that the Lord loves the gates of Zion more than all the dwellings of Jacob. (Ps. 87) They sing psalms and cry out, "My soul faints for the courts of the Living God!" Although the day may be warm and they are weary, they pay no attention to their feelings—they are on their way to the house of God, and a day in His courts is better than a thousand!

All Jerusalem seems covered with green branches and fruit. Wherever one turns one sees palm, olive, myrtle, willow and other leafy branches, from which hang citrus fruits. Even the streets are adorned with fruit. And through the adorned streets move thousands of people, each man carrying a lulov (palm branch) in his hand. All are happy; every face wears a smile. In the open places groups gather, singing and dancing. Everyone is clad in their brightest clothes and adorned with jewels and ornaments. The women wear bright scarfs and put flowers in their hair. (And all this is only the preliminary to the Feast!)

By sundown on the 13th day of Tishri, the preparations are complete. And the trumpets announcing the full moon are blown! The crowd gathers early the next morning to watch the daily sacrifice. Then there is a merry procession from the Mount of the Temple down to the pool of Siloam (Shiloah.) Leading the procession is a priest bearing a large golden ewer, in which he draws the water to be poured on the altar. He returns to the Temple and comes to the Water Gate which leads to the inner court. A great crowd awaits him there and greets him with joy. Priests blow their silver trumpets and other priests chant the words of the Prophet, "With joy shall ye draw water out of the wells of salvation." The priest then bears the ewer of water into the inner court of the Temple. Above the altar stand two containers, one for water and one for wine. The water is poured into one of these vessels and wine is poured into the other. Then both water and wine are poured upon the altar.

After this libation there is more blowing of trumpets and a ceremonial procession of priests who march around the altar waving branches. The Levites stand in choir formation and sing the Hallel (Psalms 113-118) to the accompaniment of flutes.

It is of special interest to us that Jesus attended the Feast of Tabernacles, and prophesied on "that great day of the feast," of the coming outpouring of the Holy Spirit. (John 7:37-39) On this day there was a custom of special interest to us. Using a golden ewer, the priest drew water from the Pool of Siloam, into which the fresh, pure water from the Virgin's Fountain constantly flowed, and poured it out into the streets of Jerusalem, typifying the outflowing of the waters of salvation. (How thrilling it is to know that this blessed fountain is *still flowing!* And the Pool of Siloam, buried for centuries under the rubble of Jerusalem, has been rediscovered and excavated. My husband and I were much blessed when we visited it in 1961.) Some Bible students have thought that it was when this symbolic act was performed, that our Lord spoke, thus giving them the true interpretation of the symbolism.

Shortly after sunset each night the people gathered in the court of the women, and as many as could found seats in the double gallery erected by the priests and Levites. The celebration of the evening centered about *fire,* as the celebration of the day centered about *water.* Huge candlesticks stood in the court, and so brilliant was their light that it is said that all Jerusalem was illuminated by it. Some writers say they were 35 feet, others 100 feet, high. At any rate they were spectacular.

The time for the greatest rejoicing arrived and reached its climax in the Torch Dance! It is written that "he who has not seen the rejoicing of the torch dance has not seen what real rejoicing is!" This dance was performed by the men—the most notable and esteemed men of Israel. To quote from one writer:

Music fills the air, the flutes predominating, and the men in festive array bear torches in their hands and begin to dance, waving their torches and throwing them in the air and catching them again, and again, and again! They sing and shout in praise as they dance. As the celebration continues, the Levites take their places on the fifteen steps that lead from the Court of the Women to the Court of the Laymen. They play on harps and cymbals and trumpets and sing the Songs of Degrees (Psalms 120-135.) The celebration goes on until almost daybreak. Then a procession begins with more blowing of trumpets. The Levites march across the court to the eastern gate and turn with their backs to the gate, and recite, "Our forefathers stood on this spot with their backs to God's house and with their faces to the east, and worshiped the sun—but we turn to God, and our eyes always turn to God." (This refers to Ezekiel 8:16.) At daybreak the crowds go home.

All these celebrations took place in the days after the Temple was built. There was very little recorded about the original festivities of Tabernacles, but we have the assurance that the entire seven days were spent in praise and thanksgiving and rejoicing. The last day of the feast, the eighth day, was a holy convocation like the first, and was observed with prayer, singing, and suitable solemnity.

Solomon was directed to dedicate the Temple at the time of the Feast of Tabernacles, and he ordered it to be held for fourteen days, instead of seven. "And all the men of Israel assembled with King Solomon at the feast in the month of Ethanim, which is the seventh month." (1 Kings 8:2) The description of this dedication is one of the most glorious accounts in the Bible. "It came even to pass, as the trumpeters and singers were as one, to make one sound to be heard in praising and thanking the LORD... saying, For He is good; for His mercy endureth forever; that then the house was filled with a cloud, even the house of the LORD; so that the priests could not stand to minister by reason of the cloud, for the glory of the Lord had filled the house of God." (2 Chron. 5:13, 14)

It was at this season, too, that Haggai was given his oft-quoted prophecy: "In the seventh month, in the one and twentieth day of the month, came the word of the Lord by the prophet Haggai, saying, Speak now to Zerubbabel... I will shake all nations, and the desire of all nations shall come: and I will fill this house with glory, saith the Lord of hosts...The glory of this latter house shall be *greater* than of the former." (Haggai 2:1-9)

In all these types and previews we can see a glorious picture of the Latter Day. A time of harvest is coming, a great outpouring of blessing and love will be upon the saints. They will praise God with one accord and will be built together into a Spiritual Temple which will be filled with the glory and power of God. The water from the Virgin's Fountain—which flows into the pool of Siloam—will be poured out into the "streets" of the City (Zion.) A great outpouring from the very Fountain-Head of the River of God will send the streams of salvation into all the world. (As shown in the beautiful old hymn "Glorious Things of Thee Are Spoken.") The *Fire* will be manifest in the power of the Holy Spirit, and *Light* will shine out to the ends of the earth. It will be a time of rejoicing such as we have never known even though in the midst of the darkness of impending judgment upon the unrepentant. God will "tabernacle" with His people in a new and glorious way, and will be manifested in their midst with such power that the whole world will know it. He will make a great feast, and all who respond to the invitation will be welcome at His table. The latter-day Harvest of Ingathering will be reaped from the entire world. All nations may participate in His Feast of Tabernacles. The mountain of the Lord's house shall be exalted above every other mountain. "The redeemed of the Lord shall return and come with singing into Zion." (Isa. 51: 11) Joel, Micah, Isaiah,

Zechariah, the Psalms, and other prophecies, have given us the picture of the glory of the Latter House and of the fruitful Latter Day. "Then was our mouth filled with laughter, and our tongue with singing: then said they among the heathen, The Lord hath done great things for them... He that goeth forth and weepeth, bearing precious seed, shall doubtless come again with rejoicing, bringing his sheaves with him." (Psalm 126)

"Let the people praise thee, O God; let all the people praise thee. O let the nations be glad and sing for joy: for thou shalt judge the people righteously, and govern the nations upon earth. Selah. Let the people praise thee, O God, let all the people praise thee. Then shall the earth yield her increase; and God, even our own God shall bless us. God shall bless us; and all the ends of the earth shall fear Him." (Psalm 67:3-7)

THE HARVEST MOON

When the harvest moon shines with golden glow,
My heart sends up a prayer from the earth below.
Every brilliant star shining in the sky,
All the worlds afar, seem to echo my cry:
"Lord God of Harvest, reap the golden grain;
Let Thy barns be filled with the fruit of field and plain!
Gather in the first-fruits, the cluster of the vine—
May Thy vats o'erflow with fresh oil and new wine!
"Lord God of Harvest, send the Latter Rain;
Let the rivers of Salvation flow o'er the earth again!

Gather now Thy people, and set them in array—
Glorify Thy Name! Thy great power display!
    Amen, Amen."
When the harvest moon shines with golden glow,
My heart sends up this prayer from the earth below!

        —F.M.

THE INCARNATION

Frances Metcalfe

Veiled in flesh the Godhead see,
Hail the incarnate Deity!
Pleased as man with man to dwell,
Jesus, our Immanuel.

S tars are shining! Church bells are ringing! Chimes resound in
the city streets! Loudspeakers broadcast carols from crowded
shops, and music intermingles with the roar of traffic. Lights
glow in dazzling colors! Millions hasten to and fro—the whole world
seems to be on the go—dispatching gifts and messages to the ends
of the earth. Hearts turn homeward. And all who are free to do so
seek the hearthside of family and loved ones.

To an open house at Christmas
Home shall men come,
To an older place than Eden
And a taller town than Rome...
To the place where God was homeless
And all men are at home.

How different was the first Christmas! A decree had gone forth
that all the world was to be taxed, and a man and a woman had left
their home and taken a narrow road that led to Bethlehem. O little
town of Bethlehem, "little among the thousands of Judah" (Mic.
5:2)—scene of one of the greatest acts of our great and mighty God.

Act of wonder and condescension—the incomprehensible act which we call THE INCARNATION!

Incarnation! God manifest in flesh; God in the form of man! "Without controversy great is the mystery of godliness: God manifest in the flesh, seen of angels..." (1 Tim. 3:16) This has been the inspiration for countless hymns and the theme of innumerable sermons. God manifest in flesh—essential tenet of the Christian faith!

> "There is one secret, the greatest of all—a secret which no previous religion dares, even in enigma, to allege fully—which is stated with the utmost distinctness by our Lord and His Church. I mean the doctrine of the Incarnation regarded not only as a historical event which occurred 2,000 years ago, but as an event which is renewed in the body of every believer who is in the way to the fulfillment of his divine destiny."
>
> —C. Patmore

At this season, almost all of the world pays tribute to Bethlehem. In the midst of its pagan customs and Babylonish ways, it still remembers and recaptures, at least once a year, a little of the wonder and glory of that holy night when the Son of the Most High God lay in the arms of a virgin mother. The world celebrates His birth with joyful song. And even the unbelieving repeat His blessed title in the age-old greeting, "Merry Christmas!"

We, who are devoted to Him, tune out the distractions of the world, and seek to recapture the wonder of His birth. In spirit we exult and sing with the angels, repeating the tidings of great joy. We marvel with the shepherds, who saw the glory of the Lord shining round about them, and we hasten with them to the manger. We stand with Joseph, and experience a little of the joy and satisfaction he must have known after the months of anxious waiting. We feel

Mary's mother-heart of love, and cannot restrain our eyes from tears, as mingled emotions stir within our own hearts. The great hour had come—the hour for which all Israel had waited—and *they knew it not!* But she knew! And we know that this tiny Babe is our God "Whose doings are of old," the Mighty One of Israel, our Savior, our King! And we fall before Him!

We worship... we wait... and begin to grasp a little of the mystery of the incarnation. We realize that before the creation of the world this plan of incarnation existed in the mind of God. Then God made known His plan to Eve, and gave the promise of its fulfillment. (Gen. 3:15) This promise was renewed to His people, generation after generation. At length the promise was fulfilled. The incarnation became a historical fact which the Church confesses, and the world acknowledges. But it is more than a historical fact. There is a sense in which it becomes a *present, living reality* to every true believer.

> "'Glorify and bear God in your body.' (1 Cor. 6:20) The incarnation is a present reality, and the true Church attaches great importance to the preservation of the purity of the body, the temple of God. For the complete satisfaction of God's desire was not attained in the mere creation of the human body. It is in His union and conjunction with it that God finds His final perfection and felicity."
>
> —C. Patmore

We know that the purpose of our Lord's first coming was fully accomplished: that He was "born to raise the sons of earth, born to give them second birth." And that the consummation of their second birth will be manifest at the time of His second coming, when He shall appear in the many-membered body of the redeemed.

"But we know that when He shall appear, we shall be like Him; for we shall see Him as He is." (1 John 3:2)

"For the earnest expectation of the creature waiteth for the manifestation of the sons of God." (Romans 8:19)

In them He will display His grace and power and glory throughout all eternity. This will be the *consummation* of the incarnation!

In view of this fact, it is not surprising that the early church commemorated our Lord's first coming by looking forward to His second advent. They adored the Babe of Bethlehem as "the firstborn of many brethren," and realized that His coming was the culmination of centuries of prophetic utterance and expectation. This "Rod out of the stem of Jesse" (Isa. 11:1) was the glorious Branch, the full flowering of the faith of God's chosen race. The plan of God came to the hour of promised performance! Our God is a God of performance. Abraham, the father of the faithful, "staggered not at the promise of God through unbelief; but was strong in faith, giving glory to God and being fully persuaded that what He had promised, He was able also to perform." (Rom. 4:20-21) Likewise, Elizabeth cried out to Mary, the chosen vessel of grace, "Blessed is she that believed: for there shall be a performance of those things which were told her from the Lord." (Lk.1:45) Immutable is the law of God: "According to your *faith* be it unto you." (Matt. 9:29)

As God dealt with His chosen race, so He deals with each of His redeemed. His incarnation in the individual begins with the new birth in Christ and continues on until He has subdued and redeemed the believer—spirit, soul, mind, and body. What a glorious and great salvation is begun in us!

"He that hath begun a good work in you will perform it until the day of Jesus Christ." (Philippians 1:6)

Each individual vessel of God passes through cycles of experiences somewhat similar to those of His people Israel, and of His chosen vessel, Mary. Following the initial rebirth, there come times of revelation—an illumination about the plan and purpose of God for the individual's life. Many other cycles follow. These cycles may combine or overlap, and certainly the Lord deals with His chosen vessels in a great variety of ways. But, on the whole, each individual son will experience many different cycles during his years of preparation "until we all come in the unity of faith, and of the knowledge of the Son of God, unto a perfect man, unto the measure of the stature of the fullness of Christ." (Eph. 4:13) We might sum them up in the order in which the Holy Spirit revealed them to me at a time when I was pondering these things in my heart.

REVELATION

EXPECTATION

PREPARATION

PROCLAMATION

SEPARATION

CONFIRMATION

EXALTATION

HUMILIATION

DEPRIVATION

MANIFESTATION

IMMOLATION

GLORIFICATION

UTTERMOST SALVATION

CONSUMMATION

This pattern was carried out in Israel and in the manifestation of God in Jesus Christ. It was wrought in Mary as she carried Him in her own body and gave Him birth. Somewhere in these cycles you will be able to trace your own experiences, if you are in the process of being brought into the "fullness of the stature of Christ." The new birth is only the beginning. The *Word* must become *flesh* in you and in me, and His very nature must be wrought in us. This explains the years of testing and waiting, the seasons of pain and preparation, the postponed consummation of His fullness and glory, for which we yearn with ever-increasing desire.

God has a great plan for us. He has given unto us "exceedingly great and precious promises whereby we may become partakers of the divine nature." (2 Pet. 1:4) He has covenanted with us that there shall be a *performance* of these promises, and that we shall be conformed to the image of His Son, and that His Son shall be manifest in us. "O Lord, hasten Thy Word to perform it."

REVELATION

"Surely the Lord God will do nothing, but He revealeth His secret unto His servants the prophets." (Amos 3:7)

After a soul is born again, if he continues to seek the will of God and to obey His word, there will come an hour of revelation when the Holy Spirit will begin to unveil God's plan for the individual's life. With heavenly light He will shine into the heart and mind, quickening the spirit of man to understand and believe supernatural truths. There will come a consciousness of God-appointed destiny, and a desire to find that perfect will of God. The time comes when the soul begins to grasp the overwhelming reality of the indwelling Christ. "Christ in you, the hope of Glory." (Col. 1:27)

> I am in Christ, and Christ is in me.
> O what a wonder, what a mystery!
> That I am in Christ and Christ is in me
> For time and for eternity.

The revelation of the coming of the Son of God in flesh was given first to Eve. (Gen. 3:15) She was the first to testify of her faith in it. To her, it was a *present reality*. She expected it to be fulfilled in her firstborn. In Genesis 4:1, Eve says, "I have gotten a man from the Lord." And so she had! But the redeeming Son of God was not to be born until centuries later... and of another woman! Enoch testified of the God-man to come.

"And Enoch also, the seventh from Adam, prophesied of these, saying, Behold, the Lord cometh with ten thousands of His saints..." (Jude 1:14)

Abraham hailed His day from afar and gave living evidence of his faith in the God who raises the dead, by being willing to offer his own firstborn son of promise to God as a living sacrifice. Moses built a tabernacle and put his revelation of Christ into a concrete form, showing His redemption aforetime by means of types. Yes, the holy prophets in whom "the Spirit of the Messiah" testified aforetime, all spoke of Him. And to each, no doubt, He was a present reality, for with God there is no past or future, only the eternal now.

To each of us comes that first great hour of revelation. Time ceases to be and the wonder of Christ incarnate in us becomes a burning, living reality. However, many mistake *revelation* for *manifestation* or even for *consummation*; and fail to realize that many operations of faith and grace must be wrought within us before the promise can be fulfilled.

Revelation is but the preliminary work of the Holy Spirit for the purpose of awakening us, quickening us, and bringing us into the realization of the meaning of His promises, and showing us beforehand things to come. As wonderful as it is, that first hour of revelation must pass. We cannot go on living in it, glorying in it. It must give place to the exercise of faith, obedience, and suffering. "Though He were a Son, yet learned He obedience by the things which He suffered." (Heb. 5:8) This is the meaning of the word, "Many are called, but few are chosen." (Matt. 22:14) Only the "called, chosen and faithful" will be found among the *overcomers*. (Rev. 17:14)

"For we are made partakers of Christ, if we hold the beginning of our confidence steadfast unto the end." (Hebrews 3:14)

EXPECTATION

The hour of revelation extends into the period of expectation in the believer's heart. Those who mix the Word with faith find a growing sense of anticipation. This period may last for days, weeks, years, or, as in the case of many, for a lifetime. With Israel, it was prolonged through centuries. We read concerning Abraham, "And so, after he had patiently endured, he obtained the promise." (Heb. 6:15) Yet, even then, it was not the fullness of the promise; for it was Jesus, not Isaac, through whom the promise was to be completely fulfilled. Let us be "followers of them who through faith and patience inherit the promises." (Heb. 6:12)

This spirit of expectation was kept alive in Israel by recounting the words of the prophets, and by the revelations which had been given to them at times of heavenly visitation. The hope of the Messiah's coming survived through centuries of oppression and darkness. The daughters of Eve, and their daughters' daughters, generation after generation, cherished the hope of becoming the mother of the promised Messiah. But the "fullness of time" did not come for nearly four thousand years.

In like manner, each of us has watched his own bright revelations fade. At times the heavenly vision seems dim and unreal. It is then that faith arises to carry the torch, and the Spirit comes to our aid by reviving hope and expectation within our breasts; we focus our attention again upon the written Word—those portions, in particular, which had been quickened to us on the Mount of Vision. Praise God! We have a hope that is steadfast and sure, and an expectation that shall not be cut off. If we doubt or faint and give up, there is great loss to us and to the kingdom of our God. This prolonged time of waiting, hoping, expecting, is all a part of the great plan of God.

"Unto them that *look for Him* shall He appear the second time, without sin unto salvation." (Hebrews 9:28)

PREPARATION

We little realize the extent of the preparation which must take place in us before we become able to receive the fulfillment of His promised Presence. Little by little the need for it is made plain, and the Holy Spirit gently leads us in this preparation. Moses caught this vision in the midst of his triumphant song: "...He is my God, and I will prepare Him an habitation." (Ex. 15:2)

Again and again the cry, "Prepare!" rings out in the Old Testament. And the New Testament gives us much instruction about the preparation we need. Discipline must become a voluntary submission on our part, an acknowledgment of the need for our further refining and subduing and enlarging, so that we might be fit vessels for the King's use. Every man and woman who has been called and used of God to any extent has passed through a period of discipline and preparation before the great effulgent hour came. And it is certain that this will be true of each of us; that there must be much preparation wrought in us before we come forth in that choice company, "prepared as a bride adorned for her husband." (Rev. 21:2) This is the day of our preparation.

ANNUNCIATION

The Annunciation is a scene invested with great beauty and glory by artists, poets and preachers. Human imagination comes into full play in regard to such an event as the appearing of a great archangel to a humble village maiden. How we wish that the Word of God had told us more about this amazing visitation. Tradition has much to say about Mary's lifelong preparation for this hour. We cannot verify this in Scripture, but we feel certain that God must have carefully prepared His chosen vessel for this transcendent hour and mission.

If John the Baptist, Christ's forerunner, was "filled with the Holy Ghost from his mother's womb" (Lk. 1:15), as the Scriptures declare, and if Jeremiah, likewise, was so set apart (Jer. 1:5), we may rest assured that Mary was carefully prepared from her early childhood. At times there comes to us the consciousness that we, too, have been in a lifelong preparation. As David expressed it, "Thou hast possessed my reins, Thou hast covered me in my mother's womb." (Ps. 139:13)

If the Annunciation occurred at the time the formal Church still celebrates it, it was at the vernal equinox—the birth of Spring, the time when all nature awakens from the sleep of death. "...The rain is over and gone; the flowers appear on the earth..." (Song of Sol. 2:11-12). Springtime Lovetime! If, as some authorities contend, it occurred at another season, it was, nevertheless, springtime, lovetime, in Mary's heart!

We too experience these times of love and favor when heaven stoops to earth, and we feel that "the time of the singing of birds has come." (Song of Sol. 2:12) For Mary, the bestowal of God's favor was the greatest and most overwhelming experience which could come to a woman. Countless women had aspired to this high honor of bearing the Messiah. And now, the One for Whom Israel had waited through the centuries was to be incarnated in human flesh and to appear openly as a man among men—IMMANUEL! None other than the archangel Gabriel was dispatched from heaven with the wondrous tidings: "Hail, thou that art highly favored, the Lord is with thee, blessed art thou among women." (Luke 1:28)

The "set time to favor Zion" had come; Jehovah had made His choice—"a virgin named Mary... of the house and lineage of David." Her response befitted her high honor, and indicated a heart prepared and filled with grace: "Behold the handmaid of the Lord, be it unto me according to Thy word." (Lk. 1:38) There was no trace of self-gratification or personal exaltation. At her word of submission, the Most High overshadowed her, and He, Who was the greatest of all the heavenly host, emptied Himself and became the least. He, in Whom all may safely hide, hid Himself away in the secret chamber of a weak earthen vessel.

Let us who desire to follow Him into full sonship realize that the pattern—the WAY into that sonship—is revealed clearly in the second chapter of Philippians. "Let this mind be in you, which was also in Christ Jesus, who, being in the form of God, thought it not robbery to be equal with God, but made Himself of *no reputation*, and took upon Him the form of a *servant*, and was made in the likeness of men; and being found in fashion as a man, He humbled Himself and became obedient unto death, even the death of the cross." (Philippians 2:5-8)

We too must empty, humble ourselves and take the place of a servant—a love-slave—and be willing to enter into self-death, taking up our cross and following Him. We must be willing to lay down our lives literally too, if this be His Will. Our beloved Lord and Forerunner has made the pattern so plain that none need miss the way. No other way will be proffered. Behold the humiliation our Lord demonstrated in becoming the lowly and despised "seed of the woman!"

Has the hour of heavenly annunciation come to you? Have angelic witnesses been sent to declare His favor? Has He made it known that He desires to take up His abode in the earth in you, in an incarnation of His Nature and Name? If so, you are able to understand and to appreciate the wonder of that glorious hour when Gabriel announced the birth of God's Son. And, if you are fitting into the pattern, you have responded with all your heart, "Be it unto me, according to Thy Word."

SEPARATION

"And Mary arose and went into the hill country with haste." (Lk. 1:39) She fled at once to those whom God had already visited and prepared. According to the word of Gabriel, her cousin Elizabeth was also to bear a child. It was to her house that Mary went. Out of all Israel, Elizabeth and Zecharias were the only ones who were prepared to receive Mary, and to understand the miracle which had taken place within her. They too had received an angelic visitation and had been separated unto God for the manifestation of His power. Heavenly annunciation inevitably leads to separation—sometimes even from those who are close in the Lord. This separation was soon to become a painful thing to Mary's tender heart. It was the beginning of a lonely life; from thenceforth she was separated from her former associates. This experience of separation is shared, to some extent at least, by all who are set apart for a special manifestation of Christ. There are few to understand or accept that which the Holy Spirit has wrought within them. Each of His chosen will experience a "fleeing" from the world and finding a "hill country" where a few faithful ones, with whom God has already established His covenant, will give them refuge.

CONFIRMATION

"And it came to pass, that, when Elisabeth heard the salutation of Mary, the babe leaped in her womb; and Elisabeth was filled with the Holy Ghost: and she spake out with a loud voice, and said, Blessed art thou among women, and blessed is the fruit of thy womb. And whence is this to me, that the mother of my Lord should come to me? For, lo, as soon as the voice of thy salutation sounded in mine ears, the babe leaped in my womb for joy. And *blessed* is *she* that *believed*: for there shall be a *performance* of those things which were told her from the Lord." (Luke 1:41-45)

A confirmation! Given by the Spirit of God through mortal lips. A babe leaped! A woman spoke! "In the mouths of two or three witnesses shall every word be established." How Mary's heart leaped in response to this reassuring word! Elizabeth was a highly esteemed kinswoman; and her advanced years gave added authority and strength to her word. No doubt Mary had undergone a sore trial of faith after the departure of Gabriel. We may assume this, knowing that whatever God does in any human vessel requires not only submission, but a trial of faith regarding the Word God has spoken.

For each Mary-heart in the earth, God has an Elizabeth somewhere, through whom the Holy Ghost will speak a confirming word at the appointed hour. How beautiful and stirring was the prophetic word uttered by Elizabeth to Mary! A prelude to the Magnificat!

EXALTATION

Not only did Mary's heart leap—it soared as she magnified God and was lifted to a state of exaltation in Him. "My soul doth magnify the Lord, and my spirit hath rejoiced in God my Savior." (Luke 1:46,47)

In many ways, Mary's song (which we call the Magnificat), was the high point of her earthly joy and glory. For a short season she rose into a realm of pure exultation. She knew as she was known! She saw with the eyes of the Living Creatures! She looked forward to the generations to come, and, with amazement, beheld their veneration and tribute. "Behold, from henceforth all generations shall call me blessed." (Lk. 1:48) Eternity rolled back like a scroll. Fear, pain and darkness fled away before the brightness of the Eternal One. In this high hour, strength was given to her for the cruel days ahead, and grace to bear her burden of sorrow and shame. Indeed, all generations *have* called her blessed; but *not* the one in which she lived!

Although none of us may know the same degree of exaltation that Mary knew in that hour, yet we too enter into times of spiritual rapport and joy as we praise and magnify the same Lord and God. And we need these glorious times, so that we may be able to bear the inevitable rejection and reproach which is the portion of those who are set apart for God's "peculiar" purposes.

HUMILIATION

Mary abode with Elizabeth about three months, then returned to her own house for the next phase of the cycle, humiliation. How sudden was this plunge into shame, suspicion and anxiety! From high honor to ignominy is a drastic descent. From that hour Mary was never again entirely free from stigma and reproach. Her good was "evil spoken of" not only for a few days or months, but for a lifetime. Hers was one of the most painful crucibles known to woman or man—shame. Stripped of her reputation, her name a byword, there would never again be complete escape from reproach. Her Child, too, would bear this stigma to the grave. Accompanying this humiliation were tormenting fears. Joseph, the dearest on earth to her, might well turn against her, and their love be completely destroyed. Neither was Mary ignorant of the law—a horrible death by stoning could be her fate. (Years later, when a woman taken in adultery was brought to our Lord, we wonder if He thought of His own dear mother and of her narrow escape from such a death.)

Obedience to the call of God often brings heartbreak to those whom we love most. But a broken heart is an acceptable sacrifice, and often results in intervention. It was at this point that God broke through the clouds of doubt and suspicion. While Joseph was pondering what steps to take, "...behold, the angel of the Lord appeared unto him in a dream, saying, Joseph, thou son of David, fear not to take unto thee Mary thy wife: for that which is conceived in her is of the Holy Ghost. And she shall bring forth a son, and thou shalt call His Name Jesus; for He shall save His people from their sins." (Matthew 1:20-21)

It is wonderful that Joseph, too, had a believing heart. He chose to share Mary's bittersweet cup, and thus became a partaker not only of her blessing, but also of her shame. He identified himself with her in her humiliation, and carried the reproach of it with him to the grave.

If the Father permits us to taste of the cup of humiliation, let us humble ourselves under His mighty hand. He will be faithful to defend us, and to intervene in our darkest hour when all seems lost. We too shall find fellowship with those who, like Joseph, are willing to share reproach and shame.

"Blessed are ye, when men shall revile you, and persecute you, and shall say all manner of evil against you falsely, for My sake. Rejoice and be exceeding glad, for great is your reward in heaven." (Matthew 5:11,12)

DEPRIVATION

Deprived of the respect and understanding of her friends, appearing to be stripped of righteousness and virtue, how great was Mary's poverty of spirit. "Blessed are the poor in spirit." (Matt. 5:3) Added to this was her actual poverty in material goods. Her lot was cast among the poor. And when her hour of need drew near, she was even deprived of the warmth and protection of her little home which, humble as it was, offered her comforting shelter.

Sometimes it becomes our privilege to share her homeless state, her rough and uncomfortable journey along crowded roads, her lack of the common necessities of life; but few of us appreciate it fully.

A decree had gone forth out of Rome, and God did not spare Mary and Joseph from obeying it, in spite of their high calling. And God, who did not spare Mary, did not spare His Son when His hour came, as we well know! Nor does He spare His called and chosen ones today! They too often experience poverty and suffer loss as they obey the Will of the Father. "The Son of man hath not where to lay His head." (Matt. 8:20) The apostle Paul could boldly say: "My God shall supply all your needs..." (Phil. 4:19) But he also knew what it was to be homeless, shipwrecked, hungry. He actually learned to take pleasure in necessities and the vicissitudes of life. (2 Cor. 12:10) Blessed are they who are not offended in times of testing, when they too have a taste of poverty, homelessness and deprivation.

It is needless to repeat the familiar story of the journey to Bethlehem. There is no evidence of angelic escort, nor of miraculous manifestation of provision. Apparently, Mary was dependent upon the human love and kindness of Joseph to sustain her, and a little beast of burden to carry her. Then, at the journey's end, came the urgent need and there was no room at the inn! So it came to pass that the Son of the Highest was cradled with the lowliest, and began His earthly life in poverty and in humility. He has a way of repeating this pattern, age after age. How often He tabernacles with those who are not only poor in spirit, but also poor in this world's goods.

"Hath not God chosen the poor of this world rich in faith, and heirs of the kingdom which He hath promised to them that love Him?" (James 2:5)

"And Jesus lifted up His eyes on His disciples and said, Blessed be ye poor; for yours is the Kingdom of God." (Luke 6:20)

"Blessed are the poor in spirit; for theirs is the kingdom of heaven." (Matthew 5:3)

MANIFESTATION

At last the hour came for His manifestation. Wonderful! Beyond all comprehension! Only by the Holy Spirit are we able to grasp the reality and significance of the incarnation—and then, only in part! This birth was also a death and a wedding! Divinity stooped to wed humanity! For Mary and Joseph, it was an hour of glory which could never be dimmed in their memories. Here He was—Mary's little Son—flesh of her flesh, born of her, in the likeness of man. And He is born in each of us, and appears again and again in our human bodies! Here is a great and awesome mystery—the beginning of the manifestation of the God-race—the sons of God! It would seem that from the hour of His birth the deliverance of Israel would have been manifest. But not so! In spite of this wonderful event—this incarnation of God in flesh—there was no immediate salvation wrought, except in a few believing hearts. Instead, there was a short time of rejoicing and worshipping, then another decree—this time from Herod! There followed a reign of death and terror! A sudden flight to an alien land! And another wait of thirty long years before His open and full manifestation as our Savior and Messiah.

How clearly this pattern has been followed in many of our lives. We too have known the glorious wonder of His incarnation within us; we have witnessed the manifestation of His deity and glory. We too have hoped that from that hour great salvation and deliverance would be wrought in many. But, unexpectedly, perhaps, there has come a sudden attack by Satan, a warning to flee and to hide in Egypt. We have discovered that not only must He be *incarnate* in us as a *babe,* but also that *He must come to full stature* before He can be openly manifest as a *man-child.*

IMMOLATION

In the midst of the manifestation of His power in us, we must be prepared for the next phase in this God-ward cycle—immolation. His life became a living sacrifice from the moment He wrought His first miracle at Cana of Galilee. And, at the end, He laid down His physical life as well—a complete offering unto God. He was the saving Victim of God, the meal-offering, the drink-offering—all offerings combined in one. There is a sense in which He continues His life on earth in each one who receives Him and yields to Him. And, in a measure, each becomes a living sacrifice unto God.

"I beseech you therefore, brethren, by the mercies of God, that ye present your bodies a living sacrifice, holy, acceptable unto God, which is your reasonable service." (Romans 12:1)

"Always bearing about in the body the dying of the Lord Jesus, that the life also of Jesus might be made manifest in our body." (2 Corinthians 4:10)

"As it is written, for Thy sake we are killed all the day long; we are accounted as sheep for the slaughter." (Romans 8:36)

Some are called upon to lay down their physical lives also. Zechariah speaks of the "flock of the slaughter"—the finest of the sheep. (Zech. 11:4,7) And this is the same "little flock" to which Jesus promised the kingdom. To ask for His manifestation is to ask for self-immolation.

GLORIFICATION

What a joyous assurance is given to us of the final glorification of those in whom our Lord has taken up His abode.

"For whom He did foreknow, He also did predestinate to be conformed to the image of His Son, that He might be the firstborn among many brethren. Moreover whom He did predestinate, them He also called: and whom He called, them He also justified: and whom He justified, them He also glorified." (Romans 8:30)

From time to time He gives us little glimpses and earnests of the glorified state into which we shall be taken when He has wrought these various phases of incarnation in us. We shall have a body like His own glorious resurrection body! We shall have a nature, perfect and holy as His own! We shall be raised up together with Him! So, "That in the ages to come He might show the exceeding riches of His grace in His kindness toward us through Christ Jesus." (Ephesians 2:7)

UTTERMOST SALVATION

Between the time of Jesus' birth and His public manifestation and ministry, there were years of growth and preparation. And it is likely that we shall find it to be the same. *Growth* requires *time*. God does not hurry when He is preparing a chosen vessel of grace. Though Christ be formed in us of a truth, and though we be fully aware of it, yet there is a "hiding of His power" until that great day of uttermost salvation when our God shall appear openly in those who have come to the fullness of the stature of Christ.

"Blessed be the God and Father of our Lord Jesus Christ, who, according to His abundant mercy, hath begotten us again unto a living hope by the resurrection of Jesus Christ from the dead, to an inheritance incorruptible, and undefiled, and that fadeth not away, *reserved* in heaven for you, who are kept by the power of God through faith unto *salvation* ready to be revealed in the last time." (1 Peter 1:3-5)

It is then that He will do His greater works. He will gather His great harvest from every nation. He will appear TO His elect ones, then IN them, before the great *Parousia* occurs. (The Greek term *parousia* is often translated "coming," but it is more correctly translated "presence.")

CONSUMMATION

We shall be presented unto Him, "A glorious church, not having spot or wrinkle, or any such thing; but that it should be holy and without blemish." (Ephesians 5:27)

And so shall we ever be with the Lord. At home! As one! Joint heirs with Christ in the kingdom of our Father! Manifest sons of God! This, then, is the ultimate purpose of the incarnation.

"To make all men see what is the fellowship of the mystery, which from the beginning of the world hath been hid in God, who created all things by Jesus Christ, to the intent that now unto the principalities and powers in heavenly places might be known by the church the manifold wisdom of God." (Ephesians 3:9,10)

"Now unto Him that is able to keep you from falling, and to present you faultless before the presence of His glory with exceeding joy, to the only wise God, our Savior, be glory and majesty, dominion and power, both now and ever. Amen." (Jude 1:24,25)

GOD'S ANGELS

Frances Metcalfe

PREFACE

There is one particular season during the year when angels emerge from their vale of obscurity and assume an active role in the lives of mortals. Their radiant likenesses suddenly appear in public places, and we catch glimpses of their shining wings here and there among the throng. Sometimes we seem to feel a fleeting ethereal touch as they pass us on the streets; or we catch the echo of their dulcet voices in a breath of song. Pictures of angels come to us through the mail, and their presence lends a heavenly aura to the familiar joys of the season. All this, of course, is because Christmastime has come again, and Christmastime is Angel-time to all who love its story. Children become starry-eyed with wonder as, in countless school and church pageants, they don white robes and wings and portray angels in various ways—singing, blowing trumpets, playing on instruments, kneeling in adoration, or standing guard around the little King.

Even we who are less childlike find ourselves thinking and singing about angels, though often unawares, for there is scarcely a Christmas song which does not include them. So, whether we join in the stirring

Hark the herald angels sing,
Glory to the new-born King!

or in the majestic strains of "Adeste Fideles":

> Sing, choirs of angels,
> Sing in exultation,
> Oh, sing, all ye citizens of Heaven above!

or if, perchance, we turn to the meditative "O, Little Town of Bethlehem":

> Glory streams from Heaven afar,
> Angel hosts sing, Alleluia!

we are sure to meet the angels again and again! They all are uniting in voicing their praise to God for the manifestation of His love for men, in the sending of His only begotten Son to earth to be their Redeemer.

Truly, the angels played a noble and important part in the outworking of the wonderful plan of the Incarnation. We feel a sense of wonder as we recall the Biblical account of the events leading up to the birth of Jesus. And, regardless of whatever season of the year it actually occurred, we cannot help but realize that angels were perhaps more openly manifest on earth at that time than at any other period in the history of man.

First, there was Gabriel... just the thought of the great archangel appearing suddenly in the Temple at the Altar of Incense, causes us to catch our breath in awe. No wonder Zacharias was amazed and startled! And we recall the most celebrated of all angelic visitations—Gabriel's annunciation to Mary of the coming of the Messiah. Thousands of artists have attempted to portray it; musicians have tried to capture it in sound; writers and preachers have sought to paint it with words; but its ineffable beauty and glory elude human description. Only the Holy Spirit has the power to recreate this scene in our hearts! Nor must we overlook the importance of the special angelic visitation to Joseph, for it was the angel who banished Joseph's doubts and fears and prepared him to accept his honored role of foster-father, guardian and provider for the little "Son of the Highest." And then there were the shepherds who were keeping watch in the field. We can all picture that sublime scene: the open glory of the Lord, the angel who with clarion voice announced the birth of Jesus... the great multitude of the heavenly host who praised God and felicitated mortals!

Angels kept watch over the Holy Babe as He lay in the manger or in Mary's arms, and mingled their adoration with that of the shepherds and the Magi. Perhaps it was one of them who warned the Wise Men not to return to Herod, lest they endanger the life of the Child. And we know that it was at the word of an angel that Joseph was warned to flee to Egypt with the Child and His mother. No doubt angels accompanied them and protected them during the hazardous journey. And we recall that after several years had passed and the time had come when it was safe for them to return to their own land, it was an angel who directed Joseph and led them to Nazareth.

It is fitting, therefore, that angels should be remembered and honored for their faithful ministration to our Savior. The Father has committed to them great responsibility, not only in connection with the birth of the Babe of Bethlehem, but also toward every soul in whom He is born again. Did we but realize it, we, too, have been the object of their care ever since we were "born from above."

"Are they not all ministering spirits, sent forth to minister for them who shall be heirs of salvation?" (Hebrews 1:14)

Angels, then, are not just for Christmas Day—but for every day. Yet many Christians forget about them as soon as the Advent season has passed, and seem to relegate them either to the past, or to the future when Jesus shall appear again in glory and power.

The Church as a whole seems both uninformed and indifferent to the presence and power of angels in relationship to the redeemed. There is very little authentic teaching regarding them, and even though most Christians profess to believe in them, they are hazy as to who and what they are, and what their relationship to them should be.

However, there is a strong evidence that angels are more active in the world today than they have been at any other time since the birth of Christ, and that they will come into even closer proximity and more open association with men in the closing day of this dispensation. Spiritual men and women are becoming more and more aware of this, and among the enlightened we find many who have had blessed experiences in regard to angels. The Holy Spirit has opened their eyes to see, their ears to hear, and their hearts to understand what the Father would have them know concerning angels.

We of the Golden Candlestick Company have been privileged to partake of the Spirit's teachings along these lines, and, from time to time have been aware of the presence and ministrations of angels in our midst. We have tuned in on their high and holy praise and have learned many things about what our praise should be, of which we were ignorant. We have caught broken strains from their beautiful songs and woven them into our own. At various times we have been encouraged, strengthened, warned, protected and assisted by them. During the past six months these experiences have been increasing. Also, the Holy Spirit has given us frequent instruction in the Word and in prophecy concerning our angelic companions. During this period we have heard of others who have been having similar experiences and teaching; and we have received a number of letters which have borne witness to these truths. It is evident that we are nearing a climactic period in God's Time, and that He has sent forth His angels to prepare us, and to assist us through the portentous days just ahead. All glory and praise be unto our God! We have become increasingly aware that He has "given His angels charge" over us, and over each of His elect. Indeed, we feel the heavenly host often closing in around us, covering us as with clouds, shielding us from the diabolical forces now being released in the earth by the Arch-enemy of Jesus Christ. What comfort and assurance this brings to our hearts!

Because of these experiences, we have been inspired to write this little booklet and send it forth to greet you who are dear to us and to the angels!

> Perfect submission, perfect delight,
> Visions of rapture now burst on my sight;
> Angels descending, bring from above,
> Echoes of mercy, whispers of love.
> This is my story, this is my song,
> Praising my Savior all the day long.
>
> —Fanny Crosby

CHAPTER ONE
THE NATURE OF ANGELS

"Ye are come unto Mount Zion... and to an innumerable company of angels." (Hebrews 12:22)

There is no need, surely, to say to any of the readers of this booklet that angels are of a different creation and order than man. However, it is surprising that many people, even in this day of the open Bible, still confuse angels with the human race, and suppose that good people and children become angels when they die. Nor is it necessary to explain to people that there are both good and evil angels, the latter being those who fell from their first estate at the time of the rebellion and fall of Lucifer. Such angels are known as the angels of the devil. Since it is the purpose of this booklet to deal with the angels of the Lord, we shall merely touch on these evil angels in passing. However, it is very important that every believer study the Word in regard to this matter, and be forearmed against Satanic deceptions which are flourishing in the world today. These evil angels often appear as angels of light and seem both good and truthful to those who cannot discern spirits.

There is also one other point which ought to be clarified before we proceed, and this is in regard to the meaning of the word "angel." As used in the Bible, it means "messenger," and therefore may be applied to any messenger, whether a good angel, evil angel, or a human being. Because of this, there is a difference of opinion in the interpretation of certain passages in Scripture: some are convinced that these refer to supernatural beings commonly known as angels, while others are certain that they refer to human messengers. We will leave such questions to the Holy Spirit, with this comment: He has made it clear to us that both saints (redeemed men) and angels act as His messengers and agents, both in this age, and in the age to come. We believe that together they form the Lord's Mahanaim ("company of two armies") as referred to in Genesis 32:2, and in Solomon's Song 6:13. Thus, both angels and men shall bear the testimony of the Most High, not to this earth only, but throughout the entire universe.

Ordinarily, when we speak of angels, we refer to "a race of spiritual beings of a nature exalted far above that of man, although infinitely removed from that of God—whose office is to do Him service in heaven, and by His appointment to succor and defend men on earth." Not only are angels of a *higher* order than man, but they are also far more *numerous,* according to the teachings of the early Church Fathers. They were all agreed that just as the glory and dimensions of the universe surpass those of our little solar system, so the glory and magnitude of the heavenly realms and their hosts surpass man and his little realm. When our eyes are opened to the realization of the circumfulgence of God's glory in the cosmos, and we try to form a concept of the multitudinous suns and their systems which lie beyond the range of our eyes, we are apt to feel *dazed,* if not *overwhelmed.* The contemplation of the magnificence of the angelic hosts will affect us in much the same way. No wonder the Psalmist, after he had scanned the stars night after night, compared them in a poetic figure with the angels, and cried out, "When I consider Thy heavens, the work of Thy fingers, the moon and the stars which Thou has ordained; what is man, that Thou are mindful of him? and the son of man, that Thou visitest him? For Thou hast made him a little lower than the angels." (Psalm 8:3,4)

A little lower than the angels! Yet how high is man's final destiny when he finds his way back into the sonship of God, through Jesus Christ! It was to *man* that our Lord descended, and it was in the form of *man* that He appeared, and will appear throughout the ages of eternity. True God—True Man! Therefore all the angels in heaven, from the least to the greatest, follow Him in His condescension, and, as servants, minister unto men according to the desire of the Father.

We should not mistake this servant phase of their nature, as some have, and assume that angels are inferior to men, for their ministrations are of a very exalted nature, no matter how lowly the service may be. Since it is not possible for them to follow the example of the Son of God in giving His life for men, they take delight in doing all in their power to assist their adorable Lord in accomplishing His great plan for man's salvation—a salvation which angels are permitted only to "look into." (1 Pet. 1:12)

All their movements and ministrations are characterized by a rhythmic beauty and perfection of grace, and reflect the particular attributes of God which they mediate. Their obedience is instantaneous! And they delight equally in great or insignificant missions; indeed, they make no comparisons between such, since "all service ranks the same with God," and the smallest things are of eternal significance. Moving in heavenly love, they emanate peace and joy, and *make no display of themselves* in any act or word. (Incidentally, an angel of the Lord never tries to impress you with his importance—he doesn't need to. He turns your attention and devotion toward God alone. Satan's angels attempt to exalt the one to whom they appear. If a real angel of the Lord visits you, you will be truly humbled as a result.)

Sometimes we feel tempted to despair concerning the poor service man renders unto God. Even the most devoted of the Lord's servants on earth seem so full of their own words and ways. In moments of illumination we cannot help but realize how we ourselves, as well as others, fail and fall short of that perfect obedience which we truly desire to render. How often we delay to obey, until it is too late. Or we go about doing God's will in our own manner. We are prone to add to, or take away from, the message with which He entrusts us. And even our highest ministry—that of worship and praise—is often leavened by our own spirit, colored by our feelings. Yes, man at his best is an unprofitable servant! It is only when we are given an insight into the perfection of the angelic orders and their ministrations that we begin to understand how far we fall short of fulfilling the will of God. Then we cry out as Wesley did:

> Thee we would be always blessing,
> Serve Thee as Thy hosts above,
> Pray and praise Thee without ceasing,
> Glory in Thy perfect love.

"Finish then Thy New Creation!" What a joy to know that through the grace of our Lord Jesus Christ, the time will come when we shall not be unprofitable, faltering, blind, foolish and forgetful. Like the angels, who live in unceasing praise and adoration, whose every act and service is an expression of heavenly love, we, too, shall be made perfect in thought, word and deed, and shall do all things in the name (nature) of, and for the glory of God!

CHAPTER TWO
THE MINISTRATIONS OF ANGELS

Beautiful bright angels from Heaven above,
Shed all around us your auras of love;
Attend us, defend us, our guardians be,
Shielding us from dangers we cannot see.

Beautiful bright angels, we hail you today,
Beautiful bright angels, watch o'er us, we pray;
Send from above to reveal our Father's love,
Beautiful bright angels of God!

Blessed, holy angels of God! How solicitous they are; how faithfully and unobtrusively they attend us, ever lending their aid in hours of need. If our eyes were opened to behold them, and to know all they accomplish on our behalf, our hearts would overflow in praise and thanksgiving unto the Father who has placed us in their care. For He has, indeed, given His angels charge over us, as a nurse is in charge of a child, and they will not fail in any wise the discharge of their responsibility. Once we realize the proximity and watch-care of the angels, we find great comfort in their presence. Fears, doubts, and loneliness vanish before their brightness; and faith, peace, joy and love flourish.

The Bible reveals that angels perform a wide variety of ministrations to men. There are messenger angels, guiding angels, guardian angels, comforting angels, angels of birth, angels of death, warrior angels, angels of judgment, and others.

MESSENGER ANGELS

Angels are often used as the *messengers* or *heralds* of the Most High. The first instance of this kind recorded in the Bible concerns the Word which was brought to Hagar as she wept in the wilderness. (Gen. 16) Many believe that the messengers who brought the Word to Abraham concerning the birth of Isaac were angels. But since the text does not make it clear, we may draw our own conclusion. We can be certain they were angels who warned Lot about the doom of Sodom, and warned him and his family to flee. (Gen. 19) Again and again angels brought joyful words of promise, or solemn words of warning to men. It is most interesting to trace the angelic messengers of the Lord from Genesis to the Revelation. Manoah, Gideon, Daniel, and many others were instructed by angels.

GUIDING ANGELS

There are a number of instances in the Word where angels were sent to act as *guides* to men. For instance, there was the one who went before Eliezer and led him to Rebekah. (Gen. 24) The Angel of the Lord led the children of Israel all the way through the Wilderness. Not only in Bible times, but also in our own, the Lord has sent angels to guide those who were unable to find their way through difficult places.

GUARDIAN ANGELS

We have all heard of *guardian* angels, and there is ample Scriptural authority to support the belief that each of us is given at least two angelic protectors. David was often aware of angelic protection. No doubt he was delivered by the angels many times.

It is he who has told us that the Lord has given His angels charge over us. (Ps. 91:11)

COMFORTING ANGELS

After Jesus had endured His forty-day trial in the wilderness, angels came and ministered to Him. (Matt. 4:11) Elijah the prophet received strength and help from an angel when he was fainting in the wilderness, after he had fled from the infuriated Jezebel. The angel who came to his aid baked him a cake of bread and gave him a cruse of water. "And he arose and did eat and drink, and went in the strength of that meat forty days and forty nights..." (1 Kings 19:8)

How wonderful it would be if we could partake of angels' food! We have learned of a recent instance where bread and water were miraculously provided for a company of Christians who were forced to flee persecution, and would have perished without divine assistance.

ANGELS OF BIRTH

When the time arrives for a soul to come into the world, there are special angels to attend its birth. Who has not at one time or another sensed an angelic atmosphere when he looked upon the innocent, helpless face of a newborn baby? "Heaven lies about us in our infancy," the poet has said, and it is true. Children are often aware of angels, and they talk of them quite naturally. Jesus said of the little ones, "...Their angels do always behold the face of My Father which is in heaven." (Matthew 18:10)

ANGELS OF DEATH

Angels also assist the dying and lend special comfort to those who die in the Lord. We have heard many wonderful testimonies of angelic visitations to the redeemed at the hour of their death, and of the glory that came upon them.

WARRIOR ANGELS

The *warrior angels* and the *angels of judgment* form a great and formidable host. There are many recorded instances where they have fought with and for men. One of the most widely known is the occasion of the slaying of all the firstborn of Egypt on the night of the Passover. Another memorable instance was the slaughter of the 185,000 soldiers of Sennacherib, king of Assyria, when he invaded Judah. (2 Chron. 32) There are a number of authenticated reports of angelic assistance being given in modern warfare. The most famous, perhaps, is the account of "The White Cavalry" which appeared in the first World War.

OTHER ANGELS

In a booklet of this size it is not possible to speak of all the types of angels and their ministrations to men. Besides those we have mentioned there are many others who attend the redeemed: angels of mercy and strength; angels who assist us in prayer and praise; angels of song and rejoicing; angels who have charge over various activities which concern the welfare of men. The angels of God are myriads and myriads, and their ministrations are as varied as the works of their Creator!

CHAPTER THREE
THE ANGELIC RANKS

The whole triumphant host
Give thanks to God on high,
"Hail, Father, Son and Holy Ghost,"
They ever cry.

There are nine *ranks*, or *choirs*, of angels, according to the teachings of the early Church. The authority for such teaching was based on the Bible and the books of the Apocrypha which were accepted as canonical during the first few centuries. The Church Fathers were also influenced by many prophecies and revelations given to the apostles which were not recorded, but were preserved by word of mouth. We may or may not accept these things, and in any case it will be impossible to prove or disprove them. The Holy Spirit has confirmed *some* of these teachings to us and has given us insight into the hierarchies of heaven. We have therefore included this chapter for those who are interested in this subject.

In speaking of the ministrations of angels, we have mentioned only their ministrations to *men*. Properly speaking, only the angels who deal *directly with men* are termed "angels." The others are given various names according to their rank.

THE FIRST HIERARCHY

There are said to be three hierarchies of heaven, each composed of three choirs of celestial beings. The first hierarchy is composed of the three highest choirs of the heavenly hosts, namely: the *Seraphim*, the *Cherubim*, and the *Ophanim* ("thrones.") The *Seraphim* are "the living flames of divine love." They continually minister to God in adoration and love. Their singing is of the highest order, and it is unceasingly ascending about Him. Only very rarely do they have any contact with men. When the prophet Isaiah was rapt in the Spirit and saw the Lord upon His Throne, he also saw the Seraphim glorifying God. One of them touched Isaiah's lips with a live coal, and its purifying fire prepared him for the ministry to which God was about to call him.

The *Cherubim* are frequently mentioned in the Scriptures. The name signifies "an attendant at the throne," and the form used to represent them is familiar in the symbolism of many religions. They appeared in Eden as guards with flaming swords. (Gen. 3:24) Figures of them were placed over the Mercy Seat in the Tabernacle in the wilderness, and larger and more impressive ones covered the Mercy Seat in the Temple in Jerusalem. The Lord is said to dwell between the Cherubim. (Ps. 80:1) They too *worship* continually, and, in addition, share God's divine wisdom and the counsel of His will in everything.

The *Ophanim* or "thrones" (Col. 1:15-17) sustain God's sovereign power and dominion. They might be called the "Masters of Ceremonies" at the Court of the King of kings. These three choirs dwell continually in "the heaven of heavens."

THE SECOND HIERARCHY

In the second hierarchy, the three choirs are called the *Dominations*, the *Virtues*, and the *Powers*. These are said to have to do with the starry heavens. It is believed that Paul referred to them in Colossians 1:15-17. There is not much known concerning their activities. The satanic powers also operate in this sphere, so it is generally understood that these holy angels maintain God's overruling power throughout the universe in much the same manner as other angels assist in the warfare against evil in the world.

THE THIRD HIERARCHY

Three more choirs—*Principalities*, *Archangels* and *Angels*—compose the third hierarchy, whose domain consists of *the world and its inhabitants*. These Principalities (Princes) are not to be confused with the evil principalities against whom we are told to wrestle. God's Princes have a delegated power over nations and peoples, exerting His will by overruling evil and keeping them within their appointed boundaries, and executing judgments when it is necessary. Archangels are given special access both to the Throne and to men in the carrying out of the major events in the plan of God. The extent of their authority and power is not fully known, but is considered very great.

It is commonly believed that there are *seven* Archangels. And it may be that the seven angels of Revelation refer to these. Only two are named elsewhere in the Bible, but from Apocryphal and other writings their names have been traced:

MICHAEL: "Who is like unto God?" the resplendent *Captain of the armies of heaven;* the contender for the saints and, possibly, the Resurrection angel. (Dan. 12; Rev. 12; 1 Thess. 4:16)

GABRIEL: "Hero of God" the Incarnation angel. (Lk. 1) Also thought to be the keeper of God's time. (Dan. 8:16, 9:21; Rev. 10:5)

URIEL (or Ariel): "The altar-fire of God" or "the angel of fire" prominently mentioned in Esdras, as the one who revealed the unfolding of God's plan unto Ezra. (Apocrypha)

RAPHAEL: "The healer from God"—also revealed in the Apocrypha—is supposedly shown in many instances where God's healing power was shown. It might have been he who "troubled the waters." (Jn. 5:4)

REMIEL: Also called by several other names. He is supposed to be the archangel in charge of death. He is also a special defender of the righteousness of God, as it relates to men.

SARIEL: "The beauty or colorfulness of God"—he may have charge of art and music, as it relates to manifesting the glory of God.

ROGUEL: "Friend of God"—the angel of mercy. Not too much is known about his office, except that he befriends the afflicted and suffering children of God.

We have already dealt with the ministrations of angels who make up the third choir of the third hierarchy. We realize that we have only sketched the barest outline of the munificent ministrations and glory of the heavenly hosts. For so great a subject, volumes would be required. "Truly, great is the Lord and greatly to be praised. Heaven and earth are filled with His glory!"

CHAPTER FOUR
ENTERTAINING THE ANGELS

"Be not forgetful to entertain strangers, for thereby some have entertained angels unawares." (Hebrews 13:2)

It gives us great joy to know that not only has our Father given His angels charge over us, but that He also permits us at times to "entertain" them. The Bible reveals that over and over again they have been seen and heard by believers, and that our attitude should be one of *recognition, felicitation,* and *pleasure in their company.* To entertain—in its original meaning—is to be hospitable, as Orientals are given to hospitality. Therefore, we should *welcome* angelic visitation and take delight in angels' company. In the days of the Apostles the communion between the angels and the saints was close. It was because of this, and due to the possible intrusion of the devil's angels, that Paul warned the Church not to worship angels, and *not to believe any word received from them which was contrary to the Gospel he had taught them.* (Col. 2:-18; Gal. 1:8) Angels, then, are not to be *worshipped,* but they are to be *warmly entertained!*

Jesus, speaking to Nathanael—"an Israelite in whom there is no guile"—gave him a wonderful promise, which, according to the original text, was in the plural: "Truly, truly, I tell you ALL, you shall see heaven open wide, and God's angels ascending and descending upon the Son of Man." (John 1:51; Moffatt)

Surely we, too, may share in this promise! Did not Jacob have a similar experience at Bethel? (Gen. 28:12) And have not angels been seen again and again, not only in Bible times, but also in our own age? Why, then, do *we* not *see* them? And why cannot we entertain them, not unawares, but fully conscious of their presence?

We might answer this question in part by saying that we live in a world which is somewhat illusionary, in spite of all our materialism. We appear to be on a stationary planet, around which various heavenly bodies revolve. However, as we all know, our planet is not standing still, but whirling through space. It takes faith to accept such a fact as this! And the sun and stars do not rise and set—it is the earth that turns upon its axis. Likewise, we can withdraw into our homes and feel separated from the sights and sounds of the world and its inhabitants; but, actually, these sounds follow us wherever we go, and, by means of radio we may tune them in; or, with television, we may pick up a great variety of images which no one would believe exist, unless they are familiar with modern inventions. The sights and sounds and images of the *spiritual world* are even more real and tangible, and, when the Lord permits, it is possible to sense and see and hear them.

"While we look not at the things which are seen, but at the things which are not seen..." (2 Corinthians 4:18)

The more we learn to be deaf and blind to the things of this world, and the more we become dead to self and sin, and alive unto God, the more likely are we to become aware of angels. They draw near to the child-like and guileless. They love the atmosphere of sincere praise and worship. Indeed, the surest way to invite them to us, and the warmest way to entertain them, is to give fervent, pure and high praise to our Lord and Savior Jesus Christ! Praise is the universal language of heaven, and when we learn to *speak* it fluently, and to *live* it realistically, we shall dwell continually "beyond the veil"—in the presence and glory of the King and of His holy angels.

Beloved, "The chariots of God are twenty thousand (myriads), even thousands (myriads) of angels: the Lord is among them, as in Sinai, in the holy place." (Ps. 68:17) As this age is drawing to a close, and the powers of the heavens, as well as the earth, are being shaken, we desperately need the assistance and protection of the hosts of the Lord. May our eyes be opened to see, our ears to hear, and our hearts to understand the glorious ministrations of God's angels.

"And Elisha prayed, and said, Lord, I pray Thee; open his eyes, that he may see. And the Lord opened the eyes of the young man; and he saw: and, behold, the mountain was full of horses and chariots of fire round about Elisha." (2 Kings 6:17)

"BLESSED BE GOD IN HIS ANGELS!"

GLORIFIED SUFFERING

Frances Metcalfe

Wherefore, glorify... the Lord in the fires." (Isaiah 24:15) "[In this] ye greatly rejoice, though now for a season, if need be, ye are in heaviness through manifold temptations [trials], that the trial of your faith, being much more precious than of gold that perisheth, though it be tried with fire, might be found unto praise and honor and glory at the appearing of Jesus Christ." (1 Peter 1:6-7)

According to our limited human understanding, suffering seems to be the antithesis of glory. It is difficult to speak of both in the same breath, or to link them together in the same thought. Nevertheless, the greatest Apostle of them all, the Apostle of grace, not only reconciled suffering and glory, but closely united them in his own personal experiences as well. He thereby set an example for all who, throughout the generations to come, would follow in the line of true "apostolic succession."

"For our light affliction, which is but for a moment, worketh for us a far more exceeding and eternal weight of glory." (2 Corinthians 4:17)

"For I reckon that the sufferings of this present time are not worthy to be compared with the glory which shall be revealed in us." (Romans 8:18)

"But we had the sentence of death in ourselves, that we should not trust in ourselves, but in God, which raiseth the dead: who delivered us from so great a death, and doth deliver: in whom we trust that He will yet deliver us." (2 Corinthians 1:9-10)

The First Century Church, fathered by this flaming-hearted Apostle, and by others of the same heroic faith, knew how to transmute suffering to glory, loss to gain, defeat to victory, death to life! A few believers in every church age have rediscovered the great elemental truths concerning suffering and have acted upon them, likewise achieving through grace that abounding victory which is referred to as being "more than conquerors." But, for the most part, the Church of today has little love for the Cross of Christ (except as mere sentimental symbol), and little understanding of its meaning as it relates to the sufferings of the believer. Few are eager to enter into "the *fellowship of His sufferings.*" (Phil. 3:10) Nor do they understand the real purpose of *human* suffering, and the great and unique part it plays in the outworking of God's wonderful plan of the ages. The crucifixion of our self-life is vitally necessary, and this is what God has in view.

Nevertheless, the present-day Church suffers, both individually and as a Body; for suffering is a universal experience, like life and death, hunger, love, joy and sorrow. To be alive is to be susceptible to suffering. And to be a Christian is to be a candidate for the additional sufferings which have been the lot of true believers in every generation. "We must, by *much tribulation* enter the Kingdom of Heaven." (Acts 14:22) But, sad to say, few Christians know *how* to suffer in a godly manner, and, as a result, the beautiful grace of longsuffering is rarely displayed among us. Perhaps one reason we have so little grace and glory in the midst of our suffering is that we lack understanding as to why we are permitted to suffer. Because of this, we are prone to resent suffering, or to feel self-pity, doubt, discouragement, or even rebellion. How much gain and glory we have forfeited thereby!

How much joy we have missed because we did not know how to reckon our sufferings as *joy*, as did the Apostle Paul. "But none of these things move me, neither count I my life dear unto myself, so that I might finish my course with joy, and the ministry, which I have received of the Lord Jesus, to testify the Gospel of the Grace of God." (Acts 20:24)

The Apostle James likewise tells us, "My brethren, count it all joy when ye fall into divers temptations: knowing this, that the trying of your faith worketh patience. But let patience have her perfect work, that ye may be perfect and entire, wanting nothing." (James 1:2-4)

The blessed Holy Spirit teaches us from God's Word the truth concerning suffering and its purpose and function in the great economy of God. The earlier we learn to regard suffering as God views it, and to willingly accept it as a means of *grace* to us and of *praise* to God, the sooner will His glory be revealed *to* us and *through* us. If we neglect to learn how to suffer according to the apostolic pattern, it is inevitable that we shall experience frequent defeat, and that we shall be ashamed, as Peter says, at the time of the appearing of our Lord Jesus Christ.

It is evident to all of us that human suffering is a mystery, a mystery which has baffled man from the beginning. Philosophers, prophets, poets, artists, theologians, and teachers have pondered and struggled endlessly with this mystery. Few of them have been able to explain to our satisfaction why man must suffer so much seemingly useless misery. Reformers, humanitarians, statesmen and scientists have made repeated efforts to alleviate human suffering, often with remarkable success. Yet, even in this century most Christians, as well as non-Christians, are appalled at the terrible suffering of humanity and are mystified as to its cause and remedy. Some, of course, follow the example of the ostrich and try to hide from it and deny its existence, but everyone who has an informed and rational mind must admit that we are living in a time of horrible cruelty and violence. Tribulation has already come to much of the world. Satan and his demonic forces have been unleashed upon the earth, and he has been pouring out his wrath on all believers.

The suffering of the men, women and children of this generation is simply unthinkable... unspeakable! Hunger, oppression, ghastly imprisonment, torture (with many new sadistic phases), disease and misery—already exist in more than seventy-five percent of the world. Earthquakes, typhoons, floods and other disasters have become increasingly widespread. They may not yet have reached our own front door, but we know we are but a few air-hours away from them! In spite of all the miracles of modern science, social reforms, and other benefits springing out of our Christian civilization, human beings suffer as much today as in any previous generation. Modern warfare, with its mass slaughter and imprisonment, religious and political persecutions and other evils, have brought suffering, anguish and death to millions—many of whom were our brothers and sisters in Christ. In the face of this, is it not unseemly when we are upset over the comparatively minor sufferings that befall us?

> "Must I be carried to the skies
> On flowery beds of ease,
> While others fought to gain the prize,
> And sailed through bloody seas?"

Even here in our country, which has thus far escaped the ravages of war, there is an ever increasing flood of evil: crime, sin, greed, demon activity and insanity have broken hearts and taxed countless victims. And usually it is the innocent who suffer the greatest injury. Mental and emotional suffering can be far more persistent and painful than physical suffering. In addition to these, there is also a realm of spiritual suffering, in which consecrated Christians participate in the sufferings of Christ and in the travail of the Holy Spirit. Both heaven and earth are now travailing to bring to birth the New Age. And all creation sighs and groans as it awaits "the manifestation of the sons of God," (Rom. 8:19,22) and the Second Advent of our Lord Jesus Christ. Then shall come deliverance from suffering, pain, sin and death. Wonderful Savior! Wonderful salvation! But, until that time, suffering will constantly increase and the travail will become more intense. So, whether we choose to suffer or not, we are certain to share in the general sufferings of the world, as well as in the specific sufferings of Christ, if we are truly His.

In speaking of the spiritual and circumstantial sufferings, which all our brothers and sisters throughout the world are experiencing, we also must consider the physical sufferings that are so prevalent in the Body of Christ in the earth. Satan is attacking the saints as never before. We firmly believe that Jesus bore all our sins and sicknesses, in His own body on the Cross and that "By His stripes we were healed." (1 Pet. 2:24) Our illnesses may come from our own poor health habits, or from attacks of the enemy. In any case they are to be resisted and the enemy rebuked, while we look to the Word and the Blood of Jesus in faith for full deliverance and healing.

During this process we may have much exercise in praising God in suffering. It is easy to praise the Lord when He heals us quickly. But when our physical sufferings are prolonged, it is a real exercise to glorify the Lord day after day and give Him praise while we await the manifestation of our full deliverance, which has already been provided for us.

It behooves us, then, to learn how to suffer like "sons of God"—like saints, rather than in the manner of unbelievers or carnal men. For, just as we should not sorrow "as others who have no hope," neither should we suffer as others who have no access to grace and comfort. Ours should be a sanctified suffering—a "suffering together with Christ." And great grace will be given to each of us who learns how to suffer *in* Christ and *with* Christ. As we do so, we shall learn many surprising things, and shall eventually come to see that sanctified suffering is a *favor* rather than a *penalty;* a *blessing* rather than a *curse;* a *means* rather than an *end.* And what is that end? It is wonderful and glorious beyond all telling! We shall be conformed to the image of Jesus Christ!

"For as the sufferings of Christ abound in us, so our consolation also aboundeth by Christ. And whether we be afflicted, it is for your consolation and salvation, which is effectual in the enduring of the same sufferings which we also suffer: or whether we be comforted, it is for your consolation and salvation. And our hope of you is steadfast, knowing, that as ye are partakers of the sufferings, so shall ye be also of the consolation." (2 Corinthians 1:5-7)

"Who now rejoice in my sufferings for you, and fill up that which is behind of the afflictions of Christ in my flesh for His body's sake, which is the church... Whereunto I also labor striving according to His working, which worketh in me mightily." (Colossians 1:24,29)

All this is because the mystery of suffering is closely linked with two other great mysteries which are also largely unsolved by man—the mystery of *iniquity* and the mystery of *godliness.* On the negative side, *suffering* is connected with the effect of *iniquity*—sin and rebellion against God. On the positive side, *eternal glory* is closely linked with the *grace* of God, wherein *godliness* overcomes and banishes iniquity, and in the restoration, loss is turned to gain, pain to ecstasy, hatred to love, and death to life. It is certain that it takes the negative to establish the positive. If we try to *avoid the suffering, we shall forfeit much of the glory.*

These two mysteries point to a yet greater one—which we are unworthy to attempt to describe. This is the mystery of *divine* suffering—the sufferings of our God and Savior. Yes, we have a suffering God! His pain was not confined to the hours He spent in Gethsemane and on the Cross. No! He is the Lamb slain from the foundation of the world, crucified over and over again by each succeeding generation. His physical sufferings ended at Calvary; but in His Holy Spirit He has travailed throughout the centuries, for He is a God capable of grief, compassion, anguish, pain and disappointment. And the sufferings His own people have laid upon Him by their unbelief, disobedience and failures, have been even greater than the pain of being rejected by the world. His travail has continued, generation after generation, as He labors to bring forth His sons. And not only does He suffer for His people, but *with* His people. He is "touched by the feeling of our infirmities," (Heb. 4:15), and "in all our afflictions, He was afflicted." (Isa. 63:9) What a wonderful Savior! So great, so omnipotent, so all-sufficient! And yet, He suffers. It touches our own hearts to love Him, to cherish Him, and to comfort Him, for He hungers for our love even more than we for His. He is a personal God, not a tyrannical, unfeeling Deity, but a tender, understanding, sympathizing Savior. He is the suffering Lamb of God, and He will bring forth a flock of "lambs" who, in turn, will share the fellowship of *His* sufferings. And herein lies a great mystery, hidden from the *novice,* but revealed to the *mature* in Christ.

Some of us have spent many years in this apostolic "school of suffering." We want to finish our course with joy, as St. Paul did, and join the company of "mature sons." It is written that Jesus was made "perfect through sufferings," (Heb. 2:10) and that "He learned by all He suffered, how to obey." (Heb. 5:8) If our blessed Lord, and St. Paul, and the rest of the Disciples and Apostles found that the Father's only way to perfection (maturity) was through suffering, it is unlikely that we shall be able to discover some easier way into sonship.

We can do much to hasten this process of self-death, if we truly understand what this wonderful schooling entails, and then adapt ourselves to it with joy. On the other hand, we can become "problem children," and do much to hinder our progress. Here in our nation all children are required by law to attend school. Even in the case of those who are lame, blind or otherwise afflicted, provision for schooling is made. The only children who are excused from school are those who are hopelessly mentally deficient. Much the same is true of God's children. He, in His great wisdom and love, has provided for us a school of suffering, wherein we may learn how to trust and obey Him, and eventually come to maturity. We can take delight in this schooling and make rapid progress, or we can play the truant and have to be "arrested" and forced to learn our lessons the slow, hard way. Sometimes we fail in a particular lesson and have to take it all over again. But it is certain that not one of us can quit this school, short of graduation, and still expect to attain unto complete unity with Christ. How much joy it would give our Father if we became really eager for this training and responded to it with alacrity! What a shame it is that so often we attempt to avoid it and draw back from it with fear and dread.

Perhaps you who read this may feel that I am merely passing on to you the theories I have garnered from some teacher or preacher, or from some book or article. I can assure you that such is not the case at all. I believe I have been led by the Holy Spirit to share with you many of the precious things He has taught me, and other members of our company, concerning sufferings. Some of you have requested that I do so, for this is a time of wide-spread suffering among the saints.

The Holy Spirit has taught us that before full union with Christ is possible, there is much refining, correction and perfecting to be wrought in us, and the quickest way, indeed, the only way this can be wrought is through "sanctified suffering." As I hesitated concerning taking up my cross, He made it clear to me that whether or not I wished to suffer, I was certain to do so. And that suffering, borne apart from the manifest grace of God, can be a heavy, somber, unprofitable thing. For it is not suffering in itself that is efficacious;

it is *godly suffering* that elicits the manifestation of His grace and glory. And godly suffering requires a *willingness* to humble ourselves under the hand of God and to rejoice in whatever befalls us. Many who have suffered much of their lifetime are still hard, cold, cynical and unfruitful in old age. Whereas godly suffering produces a rich harvest of the fruit of the Spirit.

Faced with the choice of choosing to suffer as the world suffers, or as a consecrated Christian suffers, we have made the choice. We will gladly enter the school of suffering with Christ and try our best to glorify and praise Him in it. We will try to be good pupils, quick to learn and ready to apply our lessons to our daily lives. We regret that, in looking back, we can see that many times we have lagged instead of learned. And some courses had to be taken again and again. Others have had to be frequently reviewed. But, all in all, we rejoice with great joy that we have been privileged to follow in this apostolic way, this way of sonship. And by the grace of Jesus we hope in good time to graduate with "apostolic credentials" as designated in the fourth through sixth chapters of 2 Corinthians.

> To suffer with Thee, Lord, to partake of Thy pain,
> Whatever it be, Lord, I say it again,
> "I thirst to drink of Thy chalice,
> I long to share in Thy loss."
> To suffer with Thee, this my glory shall be,
> Made one in the death of the Cross.

SONGS OF EPIPHANY

Frances Metcalfe

The following is a collection of poems by Frances that was published as *Songs of Epiphany*. The poem "Apocalypse" is reprinted here, even though it is included in *Thru Rapture into Translation, Part Two*, as is "Little Kingdom" from *You*. My copy of these poems was given as a gift with blessings for the upcoming year of 1973 (the inscription is included below), but I do not know when this collection was first published.

—James Maloney

Advent Blessings
and
A glorious '73!
Frances & Marian

James Maloney

THE QUEEN OF DAVID'S HOUSE

Her throne was a bench by a manger
That cradled a Baby asleep.
Her attendants were shimmering angels,
Her courtiers were cattle and sheep.

Her robe was fashioned of homespun,
And she wore her jewels in her eyes:
Sapphires glowing with smoldering love
And sparkling with rapt surprise.

Give her a shepherd's staff for a scepter,
And God's favor for a crown,
And spread at her feet a carpet of straw
On which wise men and kings shall bow down.

Hail to the queen of David's house!
Thrice hail to David's great Scion!
Glory has fallen on Israel
And God has arisen in Zion!

EPIPHANY

*"And when they were come into the house, they saw the young Child with
Mary his Mother, and fell down, and worshipped Him." (Matthew 2:11)*

O you wise men from near and from far,
O you Magi who follow the star,
A ruler is sent unto Israel—
The God-man has come down to earth to dwell!
Come with your offerings and fall at His feet;
Here at the manger the Nations shall meet.

Though He is King, seek Him not in the palace;
Though He is rich, He has come to the poor;
Though He is mighty, He seems weak and helpless;
Though He is great, there are few to adore.

He is the High-Priest, but search not the temple;
Vestured in swaddling bands—come see Him lie!
He is the Prophet and Heaven-sent Teacher,
Speaking with only a baby's soft cry.

He is the Light; but the star which has led you
Beams with a glory outshining His face.
He is the world's only hope of salvation—
Hidden, and only the meek find the place.

He is the Life, though He lives by the nurture
Drawn from His mother's virginal breast.
He who has sheltered all nations and peoples
Finds in her frail arms His own place of rest.

Come, you wise men from near and from far.
Come, you Magi who follow the star.
Bring Him your frankincense, bring Him your gold,
And offer your treasures both new and old—
Fabulous jewels and redolent myrrh;
Mary is marvelling; worship with her!

James Maloney

THE BRIDE OF CHRIST

"Come hither, I will show thee the bride, the Lamb's wife." (Rev. 21:9)

You are His hidden garden, dear,
Close-barred and walled around;
His Paradise in a barren earth,
His choice little plot of ground.
And your heart flows like a fountain
To refresh the Heavenly Guest
When He comes in the cool of the day
To seek His sequestered rest.

You are His royal palace, dear,
Upraised in the midst of the earth,
Built of silver and Ophir-gold
And jewels of fabulous worth;
Endraped with velvets and tapestries—
Imports from a distant land—
Housing treasures of Heaven's art
Wrought by a Master-hand.

You are His holy temple, dear,
His consecrate dwelling place.
Here are His inner and outer courts,
And the veil which conceals His face.
And incense arises, a fuming cloud,
From your altar's fervid fire;
His very Shekinah is sometimes glimpsed
In the flame of your heart's desire.

You are His holy city, dear,
The Jerusalem from above,
The city which has foundations,
The mother of wisdom and love.
And here shall His princes be born and reared.
To you all the Nations shall bow
At the marriage supper of the Lamb
When the crown is placed on your brow.

Garden... Palace... and Temple, too,
A City! What more shall you be?
This is too much for mere mortal mind,
So great is this mystery!
But you are more than these, my dear,
For you are His very Bride—
Bone of His bone, flesh of His flesh,
Out of His riven side.

SALUTATION TO A SON

*"Beloved, now are we the sons of God, and it doth not
yet appear what we shall be." (1 John 3:2)*

Salutation, royal one,
Heaven hails thee as a son;
Hails thee as a son of God—
Born not of man, born not of blood—
Born of the Spirit from above,
The offspring of Immortal Love!
Angelic hosts are hovering o'er thee;
All the saints love and adore thee;
The Father's kiss is on thy brow,
And thou art sealed forever... now!

Salutations! In the earth
Who could guess thy place or worth?
The First-born Son was not received,
Nor was His Word of Truth believed.
So it fareth now with thee,
For as it was, so shall it be.
Suffering... death, a shameful cross;
Pangs of hell, and bitter loss;
This, His portion, now is thine—
Glory in it, son divine!

Salutation, precious one,
May the Father's will be done!
May His work be manifest,
His power displayed at thy behest.
Rise! Unsheath His flashing Sword!

Kings shall tremble at His Word,
Nations rise in righteous sway
When it dawns—His ruling day!
Worlds afar await thy voice;
Son of God, rejoice! Rejoice!

James Maloney

LITTLE KINGDOM
Luke 17:21

The Kingdom of God is within you,
Conceived in your loving heart,
Implanted with God's omnipotent Word
By the flash of His lightning-dart.
You are the ground prepared for the seed,
A small plot of dust and clay,
Furrowed and tended by His own hand
For the fruitful latter day.

Your mind has become like a castle—
All glorious within—
Set on a hill like a citadel,
And faith is the paladin.
Guard well the hidden treasures of truth,
The wisdom of the prophets and seers,
For you are a small projection
Of the Kingdom, until it appears.

FULFILLMENT

Fulfillment!
Ah, 'tis a lovely word!
After all the weary years,
After all the pain and tears,
After all the doubts and fears—
Fulfillment!

Fulfillment!
Yes, every promise kept.
After waiting, longing, dread,
After brightest hopes have fled,
Lo! it is done as He had said—
Fulfillment!

Fulfillment!
Such as you cannot contain.
Good measure, pressed down, running o'er,
All He has shown, and so much more.
A rending sky... an open door—
Fulfillment!

James Maloney

FAITH'S ARROW

Alone, I lay with quivering heart
And breathed a song into the night:
A vaporous thing, it seemed too weak
To pierce the clouds of grief and fright.

A song... a tremulous song...
Why not a sigh, a tear, a prayer?
Our God must surely pay more heed
To cries of anguish and despair.

"Ah no," the Spirit whispered low,
"Leave sighs to those who doubt and fear.
Leave tears to those who cannot trust
The One whose love is always near."

Faith knows a shorter pathway to the Throne;
She bends my taut-strung being like a bow,
Then reaches in her quiver for a song
And centers it with care, her skill to show,
Lifts up her head, takes aim and, like a dart,
Her song speeds upward straight into God's heart!

JESUS HAS YOU ON HIS HEART

Winter throws his pall around us,
Chills us with his icy blast;
Nights are misty, long and starless,
Days are short and overcast.
Not a breath of springtime stirring,
Not a songbird on the wing.
Yet there's music in my spirit
And a song my heart must sing.
Oh, that I had an angel's guileless art
To voice it: "Jesus has you on His heart!"

Heart of tender true compassion,
Heart of gentle sympathy;
Heart that understands completely
Human pain and misery;
Not a sigh but weights His spirit,
Not a tear but stains His cheek;
God of comfort, consolation,
Other solace none need seek.
Oh healing balm for every earthly smart,
This surety: "Jesus has you on His heart!"

Long before the world's foundation
Jesus saw you from afar;
Loved you, chose you from creation,
Placed you with His morning stars.
Love so changeless and supernal,
Mortal, rise to comprehend.
Tune your heart-strings to its keynote,
Join the song of never-end.
Its cadence everywhere to men impart.
Oh, sing it! "Jesus has you on His heart!"

APOCALYPSE

Out of the east I behold Him arise,
Sweeping through the everlasting portal!
Lift up your heads, O golden gates,
He arises, the King Immortal!
His wings tipped with living fire,
Are outspread from earth to heaven.
His right arm is outstretched in power,
And the stars in His hand are seven!

His feet glow like burnished brass;
His eyes flash with love's pure flames;
And His hair, as white as snowy wool,
His radiant countenance frames.
He is the first and the last,
The Alpha and Omega, the Aleph and the Tau—
Which is, which was, and which is to come
The Almighty whom Daniel saw!

His voice, like the sound of many waters,
Swells to a great deafening roar;
Heaven and earth are all atremble
And are moved as in the days of yore,
When He descended unto Israel
And the heavens themselves were bowed,
When His footsteps shook the wilderness
As He marched before His hosts in a cloud!

He that hath eyes, let him watch and see!
He that hath ears, let him hearken and hear!
In the midst of the golden candlesticks He walks,
For this is His hour to appear.
Unto His messengers He speaks,
And His tongue is like a two-edged sword!
O Living Church of the Living God,
Hear the Living Word of the Lord!

MISCELLANEOUS EXCERPTS

The Golden Candlestick

The following are collected excerpts of various teachings, prophetic words, and poems from the journals, missionary notes and newsletters of the Golden Candlestick—primarily from Frances Metcalfe. Some are in bits and pieces as the original copies are very old and corrupted, making a perfect translation impossible. In fact, some of the mimeographs are no longer extant. Still, I believe in order to be "complete" these collected works would require the inclusion of the following.

—James Maloney

O THEOPHILUS

"I write unto you, O Theophilus," for the love of Christ constraineth me to tell you that for many days our Beloved has been speaking to us here on the Mount and impressing our hearts with His great desire to arouse His lovers in the earth. He has given us a panoramic view of the vast company of His own who are spread over all the world, and we have been amazed again to see that so few of that vast throng who name His name and believe upon His Word are actually numbered among His "Theophilus" (*lovers of God.*) He showed the great awakening which is taking place now as trumpets are being blown, in assembly after assembly, announcing the end of the old order and the preparation required to enter into "the new thing," the "strange act" of the Lord of Hosts in the latter day, when He shall stand again upon the earth, and in our flesh we shall SEE God. (Job 19:25) Even in the highways His messengers are declaring the coming of the great latter-day outpouring and many of those who have not been darkening the doors of the churches are awakening unto His Day. How great a sifting and shaking is taking place among the Spirit-baptized believers, as these truths are made known, and Mercy and Judgement join in purging the vessels of the Lord! Yes, it is a strange and startling hour to many. But these things do not disturb the hearts of His beloved ones who have already separated themselves unto Him and have followed Him "without the camp." These have been sent into the wilderness and have known the burning sands and fiery blasts of the desert; they have made the long and lonely trek to the mount, and have found their way into the King's garden and have drunk of His fountain; they have entered His house and have feasted at His table; they have drunk of His wine in the banqueting house of Love. All these He is jealously hiding away in this hour of sifting and strife. He is testing His people at the waters of Meribah; but He answers His lovers in the "secret place of thunders." (Psalm 81:7) They shall not appear openly until He appears. It is not yet time for their "public showing unto Israel." But His messengers have been sent to declare that the day is drawing near.

These few—and they are few, as He has said—are His "wise virgins" and their once flickering lamps are now becoming flaming torches in the earth, as He fans and feeds the rich fires of their love. They are not concerned primarily with manifestations or gifts or signs or ministries. And they run not to and fro after the teachings of men. They are utterly separated unto the King, and He is their Head and Teacher. They have eyes and ears for Him alone. They long and seek to know Him in the nuptial embrace and union and, once having received his Kiss of covenant, they are sealed from the eyes and touch of man, jealously guarded in His hidden places of the Rock. (Song of Solomon 2:14) He is preparing them for the great day when they shall stand at His right hand in gold of Ophir—hailed by the nations—and shall reign with Him, "making their sons princes in the earth." (Psalm 45:16)

Again and again JHVH has spoken of His age-old search for LOVERS among the children of men. How few are willing to pass through the refining, purging and enlarging process necessary for those who would rise to the place of rest upon His fiery breast. How few can really say from the depths of their being, "All my desire is unto Jesus Christ, my Ishi." (See Hosea 2:16) Blessed are those favored few who have run after Him with their whole being and have found favor in His eyes. They have had glorious foretastes of this perfect, eternal union. They have indeed beheld the King and have been taken into His courts and chambers. They have received their wedding garments and have been given a new NAME which no man knoweth. They have known unutterable ingression into the Heart of the Eternal. Yet all these experiences have been in PART only, awaiting the hour "when that which is perfect shall come." His elect Spouse, His All in All, His Counterpart and Paragon, has not yet come to full number and perfection in the earth. This consummation shall only be reached through the outpouring of such love upon the members of the Bride body as shall bring them into a perfect and transcendent union with one another and with their glorious Head. Then, truly, as He is All in All, in them all, they shall be perfectly joined in one. (John 17:23) Then shall His dominion and majesty and power and beauty and glory be manifest openly throughout the universe.

Wherefore, O Theophilus, I write unto YOU, "Arise, O Beloved of the King and hasten after Him, for LOVE hath given Him swift feet upon the mountaintops. Pour out your heart before Him in love and song; cast off the heavy cares and weight of woe that dull your mind and deafen your ear to His tender entreaties. Toss your fears to the winds, drink at His Fountain of Life and be renewed." Love Him as in the days of your youth. Let "first love" flame to consummation. Your Beloved is near at hand.

Our Lover appeared again unto me and these were His Words unto me:

"Speak unto My loves in the earth and tell them to set their lamp burning brightly, for soon shall I send My chariots in the dark of the night to gather them to the great Wedding Feast I am preparing. Many have been bidden, but few have made themselves fully ready to appear before the hosts of heaven attired in Bridal array. The Nuptial Feast is ordered. I have sought throughout the centuries for My lovers. I have found many servants and friends, some disciples and countless believers; but I have found few *true lovers* who will rise and run after Me with a passion that responds to My own burning heart of love. I offer My Father-Mother heart of love to all My children, and they flee to My arms and abide under My shadow; but few, oh, so few, rise to receive the embrace of My Bosom. Few partake of the Creative Love which is the Heart Throb of the universe—the fiery center of the cosmos. Yea, I have found few mortals who thirst for this inebriating Wine enough to quaff it freely, for there is death as well as life within the cup. All other loves must be sacrificed and consumed in the path of My flaming steps. And so I call and call, and My cry is unheeded by the sons of men. O, come up, come up, you few who will venture out of the beaten paths of the lowlands; come up into the highway (the more excellent way) that leads you up, up, up into the hidden recesses of the Mount that cannot be touched by flesh—the Mount of the One who is a consuming Fire. I call, and I long, and I wait for the day

when I shall find My heart's desire, My true Bride—for the day of
My marriage tarries long and I wait with yearning."

"Love, light for me thy ruddiest torch,
That I may gaze within and see—
For, crowned with roses all,
'Tis there, O Love, they keep Thy festival.
The magnet calls the steel:
Answers the iron to the magnet's breath:
And what do they feel but death!
The clouds of summer kiss in flame and rain
And are not found again.
But if the heavens themselves eternal are with fire
Of unapproached desire (and so He showed His heart to be),
By the aching Heart of Love which cannot rest,
In blissfullest pathos so indeed possessed.
O spousals high; O doctrine blest,
Unutterable in even the happiest sigh!
This know ye all; therefore gaze bold—
That so in you be joyful hope increased—
Look through the palace portals, and behold
The dainty and unsating marriage feast.
O, hear them singing clear,
'Cor Meum et caro mea' (my heart and my flesh)
'Cry out for the living God'
Around the Lamb, the great 'I AM' (JHVH)
The Husband of the Heavens.
Whom they forever follow."

(From the poems of Coventry Patmore)

"Yea, light thy torches in the earth, O My loves, and prepare thy robes of virginal ardour so that ye may come into the palace fitly clad and radiant with the glory of My Kiss. The Feast IS ordered, the time is set, make ye ready each and all."

"He that loveth, flieth, runneth and rejoiceth; he is free and is not bound. He giveth all for all and hath all in all; because he resteth in One Highest above all things, from Whom all that is good flows and proceeds. He respecteth not the gifts, but turneth above all goods unto the Giver. Love oftentimes knoweth no bounds, but is fervent above all measures. Love feels no burden, thinks nothing of trouble, attempts what is above its strength, pleads no excuse of impossibility; for it thinks all things lawful for itself and all things possible. Though weary, Love is not tired; though pressed, it is not straitened; though alarmed, it is not confounded: but as a lively flame and burning torch, it forces its way upwards, and securely passes through all.

"Enlarge Thou me in Love, that, with the inward palate of my heart, I may taste how sweet it is to love, and to be dissolved, and as it were, to bathe myself in Thy Love. Let me sing the song of Love, let me follow Thee, my Beloved, on high; let my soul spend itself in praise, rejoicing through Love."

—Thomas a'Kempis, 15th Century

THE BURNING HEART OF THE UNIVERSE

He is the Heart of the Universe. The burning Heart of the Universe! O, blessed are you who are the offspring off this love... the firstfruits, the children of light, the children of love! O, blessed are you, the first bidden to the feast. For great shall be the victory of His love! You have not seen the end, you have seen only the beginning. These are the days of beginnings, for He has purposed that all the universe shall resound with His praise and that all creatures shall know of His love. He has set His will. His will is fixed and sure. He has given His Word. He shall gather His own in great numbers. He shall purge the earth with fire—with the fire of His love—and shall destroy evil. He shall overcome it by the power of His love. His love never fails. O, you know so little of it, just a sip from the Cup. You would be astounded and amazed if it were all told you. You could not believe it nor receive it—so great it is and far-reaching, so invincible is His love! It is like a torch that shall never be put out. It is like a sword that shall never know defeat. It is like a tree that shall never be cut down, and a vine that shall eternally bear fruit. It is like a mountain that cannot be moved, but is fixed eternally. It is like a spring that rises and becomes a river and a sea. It is like a fire that burns and yet does not consume. Israel never fully believed it. Israel never fully received it. Israel was hard of heart; and because they were froward before Him, He showed Himself froward unto them.

O My people, My people, who will believe it, who will believe our report? Who will receive it... that God IS love, love invincible and eternal? O, who will dare to drink of this cup? You have drunk unto the salvation of your souls; but what of the redemption of your bodies? What of the transformation into His very likeness? O, what of the fulfillment of all the promises: that you shall be made like unto Him; that you shall rise up in the likeness of His resurrection; that you shall be conformed unto His image; that you shall be like

Him when He shall appear, having immortality? Only by LOVE shall this be so! Only by love!

Walk in love as dear children of God, walk in love. *Walk* in it if you would be able to *rise* in it. How shall you fly in it if you cannot walk in it? Walk in it. Fly in it. O, in love, in love—daily, hourly, moment by moment *magnify* His love, *manifest* His love. It will not be easy to do so. I say unto you it will not be easy. Your way will be opposed and great will be the fury of the oppressor. Who will take this more excellent way? (1 Cor. 13) Who will take this more excellent way, going on unto perfection... on unto perfection? O, this highway, this HIGH WAY! Few have passed over it. In comparison to those who have stumbled over the lower ways, very few have chosen the high way. The saints are calling, calling to you. A great company of witnesses are watching. Their testimony resounds from the centuries past. From the centuries their words ring out, calling you to walk in this high way. O, let love be your *vocation!* Going beyond gifts, ministrations, operations, ALL—even as the Apostle has said, "I show unto you a more excellent way... Walk in LOVE!"

—F.M.

WHAT THE SPIRIT SAITH

July 1974

The Christ of The Revelation is in our midst today.
The Christ of The Revelation is in our midst to stay.
He will make known unto us the mysteries in His holy
Word.
And He will reveal to each of us the glories of our Lord.

He that hath an ear, let him hear what the Spirit saith, for there are many clamoring voices. In these last days many evil spirits are running to and fro through the earth seeking whom they may devour. But he that hath an ear, let him hear what the Spirit saith. Watch and pray that ye enter not into temptation. And over him that fearest My name the healing rays and wings of the Almighty are outstretched as a protective covering. Tune your hearts. Tune your ears. Listen and hear what the Spirit saith.

John saw the Living Creatures and elders around about the throne. John saw the multitudes and myriads of angels, the number of them was ten thousand times ten thousand and thousands of thousands, and they were all saying with a loud voice, "Worthy is the Lamb! Worthy is the Lamb! Worthy, worthy, worthy, worthy is the Lamb!" Join in that number, that holy number at the throne of God, for the throne of God is the center of your being too. You are pilgrims and strangers here below. Your permanent dwelling place is in the heavens at the throne of the Most High God. You may surround the throne and sing with the myriads on high, "Worthy is the Lamb! Worthy is the Lamb that was slain, who has redeemed us by His Blood unto God and has made us to be kings and priests unto God and we shall reign over the earth with Him."

The Lord says to you: The Lord indwells His Zion people and He that is mighty is in the midst. He will save, He will rejoice over thee with joy. He will rest in His love. He will joy over you with singing. Let not your hands be slack but lift them up and worship and adore Him who is Mighty to save, Mighty to deliver and Mighty to keep. The Mighty One! The Almighty! Magnify Him by His name, Lord God Almighty! He is the strength of His people. He is your saving health.

Even as you submit yourself unto Me hour by hour and moment by moment, I will be faithful by My grace to work that in you which is well pleasing in My sight. Yield to Me at *every* point. Yield to Me in everything. Yield to Me in every situation. Yield yourself willingly and lovingly and warmly, without resistance. Yield yourself to the blessed Holy Spirit who is faithful to carry out the will of the Father. Yield to the Holy Spirit who is faithful to overcome and to make you strong in the ways of the Lord, in the ways of righteousness and true holiness. There is nothing lacking on My part. There is abundant grace, and I am ever at hand and ever quick to answer the call of My dear ones. I am ever quick to come to their aid in moments of temptation and trial. I am ever at hand to uplift you and to strengthen you and hearten you to face the battles which are inevitable and the struggles which must come, for the "flesh lusteth against the spirit and the spirit against the flesh and these are contrary the one to the other." But if you walk in My Spirit you shall overcome. Walk in My Spirit, not just part of the time but at all times and in all situations. Let My Spirit control you and this way will not be hard but will be sweet to your soul. For the way of the transgressor is hard, but the way of the one who willingly submits unto My will is full of joy and love and grace. Even in the most difficult moments My grace is abundantly able.

I am a consuming fire. "Who among you shall dwell with the devouring fire? Who among you shall dwell with everlasting burnings? He that walketh righteously and speaketh uprightly; he that despiseth the gain of oppressions, that shaketh his hands from holding of bribes, that stoppeth his ears from the hearing of blood, and shutteth his eyes from seeing evil. He shall dwell on high: his place of defence shall be the munitions of rocks; bread shall be given him; his waters shall be sure. Thine eyes shall see the king in his beauty; they shall behold the land that is very far off." (Isa. 33:14-17) It is by blood and by fire, the cleansing blood and the purifying fire, that ye are prepared to dwell with the Living God, to behold His beauty and His glory. Blessed are they who pass through the fires, for I am with them in the fires, saith the Lord. I am with you in the fires, the purifying fires, and they shall be heated even hotter, for He that purifieth the sons of Levi shall purify His holy priests of the Melchizedek Order. He shall purify His priests. The Spirit of Burning shall burn away the dross that the pure gold may remain, yea, gold that is tried in the fire, that they may be rich in the Kingdom of our God. Do not fear the fires but welcome them and rejoice even in the fires. Glorify God in the fires, for He walketh with you in the midst of them. He walketh with you.

I make all things beautiful. I fill the earth with beauty and splendor. The whole earth is full of My beauty. O the mighty display of My power in every seed that bursts forth and springs up out of the dark ground! The display of My mighty power, for I have said, "Except a grain of wheat fall into the ground and die it abideth alone." But if it does die, it comes forth a multitude. Every bloom and every blossom shows to the earth again My power and My glory. Even in the things of the natural there are so many mysteries and wonders—in the creatures I have made, in every tree and plant and flower. There are mysteries of life and death and resurrection. These are great testimonies of resurrection power, of My resurrection life and power. These things in the earth are but shadows of the beauty that awaits you in My heavenly Kingdom where all is magnificent and perfect and beautiful and wonderful. These earthly things are but symbols and types of the heavenly. O the beauty, appreciate these things that I have given you in the creation, My handiwork. Thank Me and praise Me for eyes to see and ears to hear and fingers to touch and a nose to smell. Thank Me that you can perceive these things, these wonders of My hand, My handiwork.

I am the Mighty Conqueror! And I make My people more than conquerors. I have a glorious, victorious Name! I tell you to be of good cheer because I have overcome the world. I tell you to see that you be not troubled, nor take anxious thought for the morrow, for the morrow shall take thought for itself. And I have said, "Fear not!" many times. I am with you and I have overcome the world. As you walk in Me you will be overcomers.

The Lord is in our midst and His presence is so real. He wants to meet every need. He wants to comfort and strengthen and encourage and lift us up into a higher plane of communion with Him. He wants to surround us with a wall of fire, because these are evil days and there are many to oppose. He wants to deliver us from the tyranny of our own wills, for we are our own worst enemies. His will is so perfect. He has such glorious purposes for each one of us individually as well as together in His Body. He has glorious, eternal purposes and blessings that He is working out in us day by day and hour by hour. At times it doesn't seem a bit glorious, but we know that the present sufferings and testings are not worthy to be compared to the glory that shall be revealed in and for us. Praise His wonderful name!

What I say unto you I say unto all, Be watchful!
In a day and hour when you know it not I may appear.
Be watchful, be watchful, for My day and hour are near.
Be watchful, be watchful, and expecting Me to appear.
The enemy would seek to divert you,

To confuse you and bemuse you.
So do not be caught off guard.
Be watchful every moment of the day.
Be watchful, be watchful, for My day and hour are near.
Be watchful, be watchful, and expecting Me to appear.
All about you there is confusion,
All about you there are many discussions.
Have an eye single and a mind single,
And a heart single unto Me.
And be watchful, be watchful!

I am the Lord of Hosts! The Lord mighty in battle! I have commanded your strength. Without My strength you would surely fail, for the pressures are great and your strength is small. You are weak, but I am mighty in strength. I am your strength and your song and your salvation. I have a strong arm on which you may lean. Thank Me for My strong right hand with which I maintain your victory. It is I who give you power over the flesh. It is I who give you power over your own selves. It is I who give you power over your enemies. It is who give you power over the evil one. In the word of the King there is power and My Kingdom shows itself in power, manifested against all the forces of this earth and of the evil one. My strength is made perfect in your weakness. As it is written, "Let the weak say, 'I am strong!'"

It is I who hold you up and keep you by My power. It is My grace that sustains you. It is My grace and My grace alone that keeps you from the evil one, that you may live in this world a life of loving ministry unto Me. In yourselves you are not sufficient for these things. I keep your feet from falling and from wandering off in other paths. There are so many ways open and so many voices and so many distracting things. But I said, "A highway shall be there and a way for the redeemed to pass over." This is the more excellent way, the way of love and grace, that you may walk in the highway. It is a high and holy way. I made the way plain and marked it out with My own footsteps. My Spirit daily leads you in My paths and you hear His voice saying to you, "This is the way, walk ye in it."

Holy is My holy bride. Holy is My bride. Holy are her works and she shall stand at My side. Live a holy life. Walk in holy ways. Speak words that are holy, words of life and love. My Holy Spirit is Holy in all His ways. He will assist you in all your ways that you may be pleasing unto your Lord and adorned with holiness, for I have called you unto holiness. I have called you unto high and holy ways. The way of holiness is not a hard way. The way of the transgressor is hard, but the way of holiness is a way of light and joy and peace and love. It is a way that delights Me and it also brings delight to your hearts. For he that delighteth in Me, I will delight in him and will share with him My own delight and holy joy, My supernatural joy. It is the way of disobedience that is hard and difficult and makes your way unheavenly and unjoyful. The way of obedience will bring you forth into a large place of overflowing joy and love and blessing.

Let the inhabitants of the Rock sing! Let them shout from the top of the mountain! Sing unto the Lord, for He is the joy of your hearts. He is your comfort. He is your strength. He is the Friend that sticketh closer than a brother, nearer than breathing, closer than hands and feet. You are living in Him and He in you. This is a close communion. He is not a God afar off. He is a very present help, a very present help in trouble, a very present companion, a constant companion. He is our refuge. He is our strength. He is our light and our salvation. He is our song.

Surely I will keep you! Surely I will preserve you! Surely I will be your Light and will hold you by your right hand and guide you all your days. I will be with you in trouble. I will be with you in trial. I will be with you in the lonely hours. I will be with you in the night seasons and My song shall be with you too. I will give you songs in the night.

You shall rejoice and see the goodness of God in the land of the living. Cast all your care upon Me, saith the Lord, for I am the One who sustains you. I am the One who provides for you. I am the One who supports you on every side. I go before you and I follow after you. And underneath are My everlasting arms. Be not fearful but trusting. Trust in Me implicitly in all things and at all times. Trust in Me!

The remarkable teachings of the
Golden Candlestick begins in
Volume 1 and concludes in Volume 3,
both available now!

Please visit www.answeringthecry.com
for more information!

Printed in the United States
By Bookmasters